The Gooseberry Hedge

Growing up in America's Heartland in the 1930s and 40s

Daniel E. Hall

Outskirts Press, Inc.
Denver, Colorado

The Gooseberry Hedge
Growing up in America's Heartland in the 1930s and 40s
All Rights Reserved.
Copyright © 2008 Daniel E. Hall
V3.0

Outskirts Press, Inc.
http://www.outskirtspress.com

ISBN: 978-1-4327-2145-9 – Paperback
ISBN: 978-1-4327-2191-6 – Hardback

Library of Congress Control Number: 2008925025

Outskirts Press and the "OP" logo are trademarks belonging to Outskirts Press, Inc.

PRINTED IN THE UNITED STATES OF AMERICA

DEDICATION

This book is dedicated to my sister, Barbara Hall Kurchak (Jody) who has been my kindred spirit for these many years. She has been a great help and a constant source of inspiration. We share essentially the same rich memory bank and she has helped make large withdrawals throughout the writing of this book.

CONTENTS

ACKNOWLEDGEMENTS

There are so many folks that helped with this project that I am sure I will miss someone. My wife, Twila, was a constant source of encouragement and suggestions. Thanks to my brother, Gary and his wife, Judy, for helping to gather up old family photos and providing constant encouragement. Thanks to my sister, Barbara ("Jody"), who was instrumental in providing material and suggestions, and her husband, Joe, who was very patient in listening to readings of excerpts and encouraging me with his laughter at the appropriate moments.

I wish I could have included more about my brother, Gary, but I needed to limit the time covered from 1934 until we moved to a farm in 1948. He was born in 1944 so he was just a little guy when this time span ended. Sorry, Gary, stand by for the sequel.

My children, Sherry Grimshaw, Diane Wall, Laura Smitherman, and Bruce, were always encouraging me to write down the stories I bored them with. Maybe they thought if I wrote them down, I would stop telling them.

I need to thank my parents, grandparents, uncles, aunts, cousins, and childhood friends for providing me with such a rich storehouse of memories. Wonderful memories are truly priceless.

Thanks are given to Chris Wallwork (chris@wallwork.me.uk) for the cover photo, the Public Library of Cincinnati and Hamilton County for the photo of the Island Queen and to Ray McDonald (nitewowl@hotmail.com) for the photo of the 1937 Chrysler.

I appreciate the work done by my granddaughter, Margaret ("Meg") Smitherman, for editing my attempt at writing, and providing valuable suggestions.

Lastly, I would be remiss if I did not mention the folks at Outskirts Press, especially Rebecca Andreas, for patience in making sure that the work of a first time author could actually be published.

D.E.H.

DISCLAIMER

All of the stories herein are based on true-life experiences. However, the vast majority of them, with the exception of those in the epilogue, took place over sixty years ago. And even those in the epilogue occurred twenty-seven years before it was written. Therefore, the writer's memory required some "cobweb brushing." Some of the minor details had to be filled in; but, for the most part, the stories are true to the way they are remembered. A few of the names have been changed to save embarrassment for some of the descendants of the characters depicted in the book. However, all family names are accurate.

Introduction –
Boundaries

We all have boundaries. These can be economic, social, educational, physical, geographical, or even psychological. When I was a young boy growing up in Paris, Illinois, a very real boundary was a gooseberry hedge. This hedge separated our lot from the neighbor's lot to the east. Gooseberry bushes have wonderful berries when they are ripe but will pucker you up when they are green. Hard green ones made great ammunition for slingshots and peashooters. When picked at their prime, they make very tasty pies.

Gooseberry bushes also have wicked thorns, which helped the hedge to form an effective barrier. However, the most effective deterrent was the lady who lived next door. She was not fond of kids, and you would get a tongue lashing if you set foot on her property and she had quite a vocabulary. I had to take great care not to let a ball or toy end up in her yard. I shuddered to think of what might happen to me if I crossed over the line to retrieve it. When I had a friend over, the first thing I had to do was to give a lecture on the danger of crossing the hedge.

To us kids, that gooseberry hedge was like the Berlin Wall.

Chapter 1

On the Banks of the Wabash

I've wandered far and wide,
Scaled the mountains high,
Set sail on the morning tide.

But no matter where I roam,
In the moonlight by the Wabash,
I'll always feel at home.
                                        The Author

I tell everyone that I was born on the banks of the Wabash but that is not technically true. Paris, Illinois is a city of about 9,000 in Eastern Illinois, which, in a lot of ways has not changed much since the 1940s. It still has wonderfully friendly people and I go back there as often as I can. It lies on edge of the plain. Just east of Paris, the land becomes rolling and forms the western edge of the Wabash River valley. Paris is located about 20 miles northwest of Terre Haute, Indiana just across the state line. Many Paris residents go to the larger Terre Haute fairly often to visit Honey Creek Square Mall and to take advantage of other attractions a larger city offers.

I was born December 4, 1934 just as the great depression was winding down. My sister, Jody, had entered the world about five years earlier at the peak of the depression. Her name was Barbara Joan but the family called her Jody, while her teachers called her Barbara. This was confusing at times. She was taken aback at the birth of a new brother and had a struggle with jealousy, even biting me on the belly and leaving teeth marks. She says that she got a good hard spanking and I still tease her about it, offering to show her the teeth marks which really did not last more that an hour or so. We are very close, as we have been all of our lives. We have the same memory bank and often share memories of our growing up together, some pleasant and some not so pleasant.

Due to the hard times, my parents, Edna & Cecil (CR) Hall, lived with Mom's parents, Bertha & John Mason Jr., in a big house on West Crawford Street in Paris where I was born. Dad worked at about anything he could find. His earliest job that I can remember was at a service station where the hours were long but the pay was short. Mom and Dad kept track of every penny that was spent and had to make the dollars stretch. Such were the times for most folks. Dad passed away in 1990 and Mom in 1994; both lived until the age of 82.

When I was about two years old, we moved to a small rental house on North Central Street for a short time. Meanwhile, when the economy had improved some, our grandparents Bertha and John Mason, Jr., which Jody and I called "Meme & Me Mason," had purchased a nice bungalow further northwest. Later, they helped Mom and Dad purchase a small home just east of their house across a vacant lot. This lot served as my grandfather's large garden. I must have been about three when we moved there.

Every spring, he would hire an old man with a mule to plow his garden. That mule was so stubborn that the old man would get mad and let out a string of language that would turn the neighborhood blue. I learned a lot of new words from him, much to the chagrin of my mother. Have you ever had your mouth washed out with Lava soap?

We all worked in that garden from time to time and our grandfather worked long hours in it. It holds many a drop of his sweat. Meanwhile, our grandmother, Meme Mason, took ill with cancer. Mom spent about five years caring for her during her very painful bout with the dreaded disease. Mom had a path worn across the garden between our houses. My sister, Jody, did most of the housework and a lot of meal preparation during this time. Meme died in 1941.

As far as the garden, it was very important for that garden to support our grandparents and us because money was still scarce. I remember Mom doing a lot of vegetable canning and Dad building a big rack of shelves in the basement to store the jars. I still don't know where Mom found all the time to do what she did.

At the rear of the garden was a blackberry patch where I often played. I would dig trenches and put boards and dirt over the top to make tunnels. This was heaven for a boy, and I spent hours there.

Me Mason also had a big chicken yard behind the house which was divided into two lots, one with a brooder house, and one with a hen house. Several peach trees grew in the lot with the hen house, which produced very juicy peaches. Those we didn't eat from the trees, Mom canned. Like the vegetables from the garden, the chickens that my grandfather raised were also important to our families. Sometimes I would see him stop while gathering eggs, knock little holes in both ends of an egg, and suck the inside out for a snack. How he could stand to do this, I will never know. Once he reached under a hen to get an egg and there was a snake under her. That probably gave him the shakes for a week.

Once he had a big white rooster that hated me. I would go into the chicken lot and I would see that rooster peeking around the chicken house at me. He would wisely let me get a good way inside the lot and then come running after me with his wings flapping wildly. He would always grab me by the seat of the pants where he would hang on while flapping his wings. I was terrified of that rooster which resulted in my limited entry into the chicken yard. It was a happy day when my grandfather chopped off his head and I saw him flapping his wings for the last time. Fried chicken had never tasted so good!

Our House

Our house across the garden seemed like a pretty large house when we were kids. Jody & I had the opportunity to tour it a few years ago. We both swore it had shrunk! It was a two-bedroom, one-bath house. Jody had a very small room of her own on the northwest corner with a window overlooking an alley, which ran between the garden and our house. I slept on a cot in the dining room. In those hot and muggy Illinois nights, we slept with the windows open to catch what breeze we could.

There would be what we called "tramps" walking up and down the alley once in awhile and we kind of got used to them being there. Anyone could have reached right through the rusty screen to grab Jody but we didn't think much about it in those days. Few people wanted more kids because they often couldn't afford the ones they had.

When we toured the property a few years ago, there in the back yard, in a sidewalk that my dad had made, was my little hand-print where I had pressed my hand into the wet concrete. There was a 1938 date scratched under it. I was three years old at the time. It was very touching and brought back a lot of memories of those hard but pleasant times.

School Days

Vance School was an elementary school for grades one through six lo-

4

cated on North Main Street several blocks northeast of our house. Jody and I both attended there. She was a much better pupil than I was, and the teachers all remembered her. On the first day of school, my teacher would say, "Oh, you're Barbara's brother." I had to put up with that all through school. However, I would quickly bring the teachers down to earth with my performance.

Vance School was one of those two-story brick schoolhouses; grades five and six had their classrooms on the second floor and there was a tube-slide fire escape for them. We looked forward to being on the second floor during fire drills, a powerful incentive to study hard and get promoted. How we envied the kids coming down that slide during fire drills.

We had to walk five blocks to and from school no matter the weather. This could be very daunting on those cold and snowy winter days. I can't ever remember school being closed or let out early because of the weather. But we always had snowsuits and mackinaw coats to wear. Sometimes you would get bombarded with snowballs from other kids on the way home from school and you would be all white by the time you made it home.

Nowadays, no parent would think of allowing little first graders to walk that far to school in all kinds of weather. We never thought much about it. Maybe kids were tougher in those days.

I hurried home every evening after school to listen to my favorite shows on the radio. There was *The Shadow, Dragnet, Gangbusters, Hop Along Cassidy* and others. The radio in those days was every bit as captivating for kids as the TV is now. It was probably better for your head because you had to imagine all the scenes while TV requires very little imagination. They were always offering some deal where you would have to save box tops to send in for a decoder ring or some such gadget. I would anxiously check what the mailman brought each day.

When I was in fourth grade, I had an extreme crush on an "older woman." Her name was Martha Z. and she was in sixth grade. She was really classy but, of course, paid no attention to me, whom she probably thought was a little snot. Someone must have told her that I had a crush on her because, wonder of all wonders, she came up to me one day on the playground, pulled my stocking cap away from my ear and whispered something to me. I was so shook, that I didn't even remember what she said. She just ran away giggling. I was so enthralled that I wouldn't let my mom wash that cap for a long time because she had touched it.

Cats Galore

The lady next door, whom I will call "Mrs. Violet Fisk," did not like kids but loved cats. She had 26 cats from various genetic pools. Every evening, Mrs. Fisk would come out in the back of her house to feed all 26 cats. She would call, "Here Kitty, Kitty, Kitty" then call each one's name. I kid you not, all 26! I had her spiel memorized but couldn't put the name with the respective cat.

Cats would materialize from nowhere! They would be running across roofs, dropping out of trees, and running down the street, who knows from where. It was truly a sight to behold.

I had a nice big sandbox in our back yard which the cats thought was their personal litter box. They must have thought we were very kind to provide it for them. They always covered their messy deposits with sand, which irritated me to no end. I would much rather they would have left them on the surface where I could have seen them and scooped them out. As it was, they were like buried land mines and I would invariably get my hands messy in them. Sometimes, when Mrs. Fisk (We were taught to always address adults properly. No first names!) wasn't looking, I would throw their poop over the hedge. Well, I thought of creative ways to make a cat's life miserable without being cruel. We won't go into that here because that is almost enough material for another book. I could

6

entitle it: *101 Ways to Make Cats Uncomfortable.*

Neighbor Kids

The neighbors across the street had a girl, Shirley, who was in my grade in school. Of course, I wouldn't be caught dead walking her to school. She had a younger sister named Dixie and I think another sister but I can't recall her name. They were really about the only kids I had to play with in the near neighborhood so we spent a lot of time together. A time or two, I would clean the cat poop out of my sandbox, flood it with water, and Shirley and I would strip to our underwear and go *"swimming."* With no TV or organized activities for kids in those days, we had to be creative.

At my 50th class reunion in 2003, I was sitting at the banquet table when I felt a tap on my shoulder. I turned around and saw a guy I didn't know so I got up and introduced myself. He said, "My wife tells me that you used to fry disgusting things to freak her out." I remembered having an old skillet and cooking stuff, usually potatoes, over a fire out in my back yard but I didn't remember frying any freakish things. Although, I do remember that I always liked to tease girls and often tried to freak them out.

About this time Shirley showed up. I wouldn't have known her. We talked for a while and she asked me if I remembered taking her out in the cornfield in our neighborhood. I wasn't sure I wanted to go there but she seemed anxious to talk about it. Her husband was bigger than me so I wanted to tread lightly with this conversation. I told her that I really didn't remember, but she pressed on. Then she said that I had just gotten a Boy Scout compass and showed her how you couldn't get lost if you had a compass. I breathed a sigh of relief!

Shirley also told me that one time she was walking home from

Vance School when she looked back and saw a man following her. She said that I was walking on the other side of the street and also saw the man. She said that I then crossed over and walked with her to keep her safe. What a gentleman! I didn't remember that one either.

Dad at Work

I loved spending time with Dad when he worked at McCord's service station. Because he did not like his name, Cecil, his friends and co-workers called him CR. At the station, when I was very young, he would toss me up and catch me and the guys would tease me about flying. I was always teased a lot.

When I got a little older, Dad would let me sit at a big old desk and stamp receipts or something with a rubber stamp. I was not allowed to pump gasoline but if someone came in and wanted a gallon of kerosene, I could pump it out of a 55-gallon drum and fill their container. I thought I was performing a valuable service.

Sometimes Dad would take the tanker truck out on a route to fill farmers' fuel tanks. He would often let me ride along. If I knew he was coming by the house to pick me up, I would stand with my nose pressed against the screen door and the cross-hatching would be imprinted on my nose when I got in the truck. He got a kick out of me being so excited to go with him.

Most of the farmers would tease me and a couple of them would tease about Dad giving me to them so I could live on their farm. Sometimes they sounded serious and it would bother me. I remember asking Dad one time, when we got back in the truck, if he was really thinking about giving me away. He lovingly assured me that they were just teasing me. You have to be careful how you tease a kid.

At the end of his route, I could always count on Dad stopping at a store and buying us each a Hershey bar. That was the best tasting chocolate ever. How I would love to go out on that route with him just one more time.

The station where he worked was near the railroad depot and the Big Four restaurant that faced the railroad tracks. Sometimes, when Jody was at the station with me, she walked me across the parking lot to the restaurant where we could buy hamburgers for five cents. Later, when I was old enough to have a paper route, I would walk over to this restaurant from the newspaper office and treat myself to an order of hot roast beef with mashed potatoes and gravy. Yum!

Science Class

With our Grandmother Mason dying of cancer next door, Jody became interested in doing cancer research as a career. She threw her whole heart into it and took mine with her. Every Sunday afternoon, while the folks were napping, she would sit with me and try to make me learn a bunch of stuff about medical science. This was the best way she could think of to keep me quiet!

I got to know a lot about Louis Pasteur, Madame Currie and many other great pioneers in the field of medical research. Then came the dreaded tests and I would shudder to think of what would happen if I did poorly. Her teaching dedication would later serve her well in becoming a veteran teacher and administrator.

Her interest in medical science faded when she ran out of money her first year at what is now Eastern Illinois University in Charleston. She returned home to Paris where she was gently persuaded by our mother and her pastor to apply for admission to Moody Bible Institute in Chicago, which had no tuition fees. She eventually enrolled there and graduated in 1955 after she was married.

Chapter 2

The Hills of Southern Indiana

The rolling hills of Indiana,
A sight that you must see.

With leaves of red and gold,
Nothing is as pretty as a tree.

I'll return again someday,
And I can hardly wait.

You haven't seen true beauty,
Till you've seen the "Hoosier State!"
                                        The Author

The topography of Southern Indiana is characterized by rolling hills; which, in the fall of the year, can be breathtakingly beautiful from the leaves of the hardwood trees turning various shades of gold and red. Folks travel for many miles just to see this natural wonder. Brown County is a legendary tourist destination in the autumn. We used to call it God's pallet.

The Hills of Southern Indiana

Some of the hillsides can be quite steep which has inspired some funny stories over the years, some true and some not so true. You must decide.

There once was a farmer who had a big garden on the side of a hill. He liked to raise squash and corn but he had to plant them in a certain way in order to maximize his crop yield. He had to plant the squash uphill from the corn. When he tried to grow squash downhill from the corn, the squash would ripen, come off the vine and roll downhill into the creek. But if he grew the squash uphill, when they started rolling downhill, the crooked tops would hook around the corn stalks and save them from rolling down into the creek. Who said that necessity is the mother of invention? That farmer was pretty smart.

Then there was the farmer who had a farm so hilly that one day he looked up the chimney in his cabin and saw his neighbor out working in his field. Now that farm would take the prize for hilliness.

There once was a little town in the hill country that had a big general store, kind of like my grandfather's store that I will talk about later. There was a boy named Booger who liked to hang out in the store. Well, Booger loved mules and wanted one really bad. He talked about mules all the time and drove everyone about half crazy.

One day the store got a load of coconuts that they put out to sell. Nobody in those parts had ever seen a coconut and the customers were curious as to what they were and what they did. Now, Booger was as curious as everyone else, maybe more so, so the storekeeper told him they were mule eggs to have some fun with him. He said that if Booger would sit on one for about three weeks, a baby mule would hatch out. He thought Booger would see that it was a joke but ole Booger fell for it hook, line, and sinker. The storekeeper thought this might be a good way to get rid of him for about three weeks of relief from mule talk. So he gave Booger an "egg."

Booger was so excited and took the egg home and made a little nest for it in his yard. Then he started sitting on it faithfully. It got to be a joke around town and folks would go by his house just to see Booger out there sitting on the mule egg come rain or shine. They had a hard time controlling their laughter, but Booger didn't care because he would soon have a baby mule to raise. He would even turn the egg over every day or so just like he had seen hens do with their eggs.

After about three weeks, he picked the egg up and pressed his ear to it to see if he could hear the baby mule stirring around inside. He accidentally dropped the egg and it rolled downhill into a thicket. Well, the egg scared a rabbit out of the thicket and it sat there for a few seconds. It looked at Booger and Booger looked at it and thought it looked kind of funny for a baby mule. The rabbit hopped off and he ran after it but the rabbit was too fast and ran away from Booger.

The next day, he started hanging out at the store again; the store-keeper couldn't resist asking him if the egg ever hatched. Booger replied that it did but that the baby ran away. He said it was OK, though, because the baby mule would grow up to be too wild to ever get a harness on and, even if he could harness him, he would never want to plow that fast. The storekeeper scratched his head and couldn't help thinking that ole Booger had pulled the joke on him.

That's enough of that foolishness. Now let's get serious again.

My mother's mother, Bertha Mason ("Meme Mason"), was born and raised in Southern Indiana. When she left to marry my grandfather, John Mason, Jr. ("Me Mason"), she was teaching school in French Lick, Indiana and drove a horse and buggy to school each day. She had met my grandfather through a lonely-hearts ad, similar to what e-harmony is today. He was a lonely bachelor running a drugstore/post office in the small town of Redmon, Illinois. When he looked at magazines that came trough the mail, he noticed the lonely-hearts columns and decided to place an ad. One of the respondents was Bertha and they began a correspondence. Later, he took a train to see her and things clicked, as they say (more about this romance later). Her maiden name was Hall, which kind of made things interesting because their daughter, my mom, married my dad who was a Hall. I hope you don't get too confused about this.

Anyway, Mom had a lot of relatives in Southern Indiana and many of them were living near, or in the tiny town of Leipsic.

Leipsic

My great grandfather, JC Hall (Mom's mother's father) lived in Leipsic and owned and operated a general store there. It seemed huge to me at that time but wouldn't compare to the big box stores now. JC lived in a big, barn-like house with a big front porch and pillars. The house is still standing but the front porch has been enclosed and the house looks completely different than it did then. However, the big stained glass window in the dining room was still there the last time I rode past the house. I loved to sit on his porch and rock with him in the old hickory rocking chairs while he told me stories. I never knew my great grandmother, Laura, since she died before my time.

Once, while rocking, I saw a pretty girl drive by in a fancy red cart being pulled by a goat. Her blond hair was blowing in the wind and it was puppy love at first sight. I somehow learned her name was Ginger. She would ride up and down the street and I longed to ride in her goat cart with her but I was too shy. A couple of days later, I was sitting on the porch when, wonder of all wonders, she stopped in front of the house and invited me to ride with her. From then on that summer, I often rode with her and I was in heaven. I don't know what ever happened to Ginger but I hope she has had a good life.

JC had such a presence in the community that his word was pretty much law around those parts. He was kind of a rough and ready, imposing guy and always spun the rear tires on his 1936 Buick when he took off. The story goes that he once came home and slammed the front door rather hard. My great grandmother got after him, and said that if he kept slamming the door that hard, the glass would break. He opened it again and slammed it and, sure enough, the glass broke all over the floor. Even so, he loved his family and treated them well. I idolized him.

Before World War II, we always spent a week or two each summer in Leipsic. Sometimes Mom, Jody and I would travel there by train from Paris, but usually Dad would drive us down in our 1937 Chrysler. That was a long trip in those days. He would usually stay for a day or two, go back to work in Paris, and come get us at the end of our visit. Jody and I have wonderful childhood memories of our visits in Southern Indiana when the times seemed simpler.

It seemed like all my cousins and uncles there liked to tease me. They commonly called me "Daniel in the lion's den," after the Bible story about Daniel. Somehow, they got to teasing me about bear hunting. It could be because I was commonly seen carrying a toy gun around. Uncle Harold once said that I would grow up to be so tough that I could hunt bears with a switch. I never quite lived up to his expectations.

How I looked forward to those trips to the enchanted land of Southern Indiana!

The Big Store

JC's store was located next to the railroad crossing on Tater Road (Now CR-475) two or three blocks north of JC's house on the east side of the street. There were two stories but I don't remember what was on the second floor. At the front were big plate glass windows and there were two wooden benches under the windows on the outside. Next to the street there were three gasoline pumps. They were the old fashioned kind where you had to pump the gas up into a glass tank on top by working a lever on the side. The tank had gallon marks on the side so that you could tell how much gas you were dispensing to the customer. You see these kinds of pumps in museums now.

When you entered the store, you were greeted by a variety of wonderful odors. Coffee was being ground and crackers and cookies were sold from barrels, as were sugar, flour, cereal, and other such products. There was a dry-goods section where ladies bought cloth for their sewing projects, and brand new bib overalls of assorted sizes were hanging on hooks nearby. High up on shelves were washtubs, coal buckets, copper boilers, baskets, etc. The walls were lined with shelves completely filled with canned goods, boxed cereal and such. The floor was wooden and kept well oiled to hold the dust down.

At the back of the store was the fresh meat case with the butcher block behind it. There was always a great display of fresh meat. Farmers could trade poultry for groceries, and the chickens, ducks and geese were dressed and put in the cases for sale to the town-folk. Eggs and cream could also be traded in, the cream sold to the dairy and the eggs sold in the store. It was a store typical of those shown in old Western movies, and a wondrous place for kids.

Out in back of the store was the icehouse where big blocks of ice were stored under layers of saw dust. The walls and door were well insulated, and ice would keep in there all summer. They said that in the early days, the ice was sawed from the surface of area lakes during the cold Indiana winters. The icehouse was a good place to visit on a hot August day.

Saturday evenings the store stayed open late and the farm families would literally swarm in to buy their week's groceries. Some would actually come in horses and wagons or buggies. Some also came by horseback. Many of the men would sit on the benches or stand around outside while their wives shopped for the supplies.

They told great stories but Mom wouldn't let me hang around much out there. I never knew why because there was much for a young boy to learn from the men out in front of that store.

Saturday evening was the big social event in the town each week, and JC always gave away a big basket filled with groceries to the holder of the lucky raffle ticket. Word of who won the groceries would spread like wildfire. Many a telephone would ring with the news, along with other gossip of the day.

The telephones hung on the wall with a ringing crank on the side and, if you wanted to call someone, you would pick up the receiver and give it a crank. The operator would answer and you would tell her the number or the name of the person you wanted to call. Everyone was on a party line with a few other subscribers and you picked up the receiver when the operator rang your designated number of rings. Some nosey people on your line could quietly pick up the receiver and listen in on the conversation. This was how a lot of gossip was passed around. Sometimes you could hear them pick up the receiver, and once in a while, some eavesdropper would sneeze or get to breathing heavily when hearing the juicy conversation. My grandfather, JC, would tell them in a loud and gruff voice to get off the dad gum line, then he would hear the telltale click of the receiver being replaced on the hook.

Huckster Wagons

At one point, my great grandfather, JC Hall's son, Flet, asked if he could partner with his father in the store business. He was told that there was not enough income from the store to support two families, but my great uncle had an idea. He knew that many folks living in the hills found it difficult to get to town to buy groceries. He wondered why they couldn't take the store to them.

Flet presented the idea to his dad who finally agreed to give it a try. They bought a big panel truck, and installed shelves along the sides with little fences to keep the groceries from bouncing out when they were driving over bumpy roads. Unimproved country roads were the norm in those days.

Uncle Flet drove the first mobile grocery store for a while and it was so successful that they eventually bought two more trucks and outfitted them.

They then set up routes out in the hills and hollers of Southern Indiana and hired drivers to run the routes on most days of the week. It was an ingenious demonstration of logistic managing. The driver would stop in front of farmhouses, honk the horn and the farmer and his family would come out and buy a good supply of groceries. They could even trade in their poultry and eggs for groceries and the driver had to be skillful in negotiating a fair trade. Back then, these routes went over pretty wild country where some whisky stills remained in operation. Those "moon-shining" farmers were very sensitive about folks stopping at their places and, since the quality of their "white lightning" was a status symbol amongst the local folks, they were as afraid of spies as they were of government agents.

When Jody and I were visiting Leipsic, it was a special treat to be invited to ride along on a huckster wagon route. We would each go with different drivers. It was way before daylight when the drivers had their vehicles all stocked with groceries and ready to roll. If we were late, the drivers would leave without us. We were never late but usually arrived early with great anticipation.

On one trip that I went on, we left at about sunrise, drove on highways for a while, then paved secondary roads, then gravel roads and eventually traveled over some dirt roads that resembled lanes. We went into the wildest country I could ever imagine. Once the driver stopped at what seemed just another part of the country road and honked his horn. I was curious as to why he was stopping there. He had me look way on top of a hill where I could just see a cabin through the brush. It was in the heart of summer but there was smoke curling up from a little shed. No doubt he was cooking up a little batch of liquid refreshment. The driver honked again.

Pretty soon the bushes parted and a bearded face appeared and then I could see a rifle barrel sticking out also. The bearded face looked around and gazed up and down the road to make sure the coast was clear. He then disappeared for a minute or so then out came his wife and about ten children of various ages. One of the kids was pulling a rickety old wagon filled with vegetables, cream, and other stuff they wanted to trade for groceries. The driver did a quick assessment of the produce and made them an offer. It must have been acceptable because the whole family climbed aboard the vehicle single file. I was given quiet instructions to watch and make sure they didn't steal anything. It was a tough job to watch so many hands. I was really kind of afraid to tell the driver if I saw some sticky fingers in operation but I didn't see any problems.

The kids wanted candy but their dad said no, and I felt sorry for them because I always gorged on sweets when I was in JC's store. When they were through shopping, the driver gave each of the kids a stick of candy as they left. It was fun to see those kids so happy. Some were jumping up and down with glee. Little things mean a lot when you don't have much.

At another stop, there were a couple of chickens to be traded in. It was my job to watch the chickens and keep them under control at the rear of the vehicle. Usually there was an empty chicken crate to keep the live chickens in, but on this trip, there was not one there. We still took the chickens in trade, and the driver told me to tie their legs together and they would just sit there and enjoy the day. It worked, sort of.

On another trip, a farmer traded in a pig. He was too big for the crate so I had to build a little pen the best I could out of boxes and sacks of flour, etc. That pig was restless to say the least. He took constant supervision and I was happy when that trip ended.

On those trips, we were provided lunch and snacks, which we prepared from the shelves. There was always peanut butter and bread, apples, crackers and other good stuff. We always got plenty to eat. After all, we were JC's great-grandkids and the drivers kind of spoiled us.

Relieving ourselves was another proposition. It wasn't bad for a boy, since there was always brush along the road, but I felt sorry for Jody. You had to be careful of snakes if you went into the brush because there were lots of copperheads in those parts. If you had to do a number two, you had to remember to take the roll of paper that was provided on the truck. Life is full of little problems.

On one trip, Jody and I went together. It was late when the driver completed his route and headed back to Leipsic, and it started to rain. He drove on in the rain and then the headlights flickered out. He went out in the rain and pulled the fuse; sure enough, it had blown. He got back in and looked around for a replacement fuse with no success. He sat there for a minute and thought about it. I thought we would be stranded at the edge of the road until daylight. Finally he thought of something that might get the lights to come back on. He opened a pack of chewing gum and wrapped the foil around the blown fuse and replaced it. Behold, the lights worked! I thought he was a genius. We made it back to town with no more problems.

How could a kid have any more fun that going along on a huckster wagon trip in the hills of Southern Indiana? The huckster wagons were so successful that JC and his son, Flet, became full partners in the grocery business.

Uncle Harry's Farm

My great grandfather, John Charles Hall, whom I refer to as JC in this story, had several children. His daughter Mae was married to

Harry Parrish who had a farm three or four miles southeast of Leipsic. That farm was a magical place for kids. One of the greatest charms was the lack of electricity. It was such fun using kerosene lamps, and their prized possessions were their Aladdin lamps, which had a luminous mantle that glowed much brighter than a regular kerosene lamp. When you left the house after dark, it was such fun to light a lantern and carry it with you. After our visits to Uncle Harry's farm, I always felt deprived when I got back to Paris where all you had to do was flip a switch.

It was great fun to get up early and go with Uncle Harry to milk the cows and do other chores, all by lantern-light. He taught me how to milk a cow, and you didn't even have to pump their tails like I had been teased about. The first time in the barn, I expected to see him pump tails. They had four or five cats on the farm and they would line up behind the cows so we could squirt milk in their mouths from time to time. I really got a kick out of that. We couldn't squirt too much, though, because the milk was valuable.

They took the milk to the back porch of the house where they ran it through a hand-cranked cream separator. They always kept some of the cream in the icebox, no refrigerator of course, and it was great to sit down for breakfast at a round oak table with an oilcloth on it and pour cold, fresh cream on our cereal by lamplight. Very quaint indeed!

Aunt Mae had an iron stove that was heated with coal or wood. It had a water reservoir on the side out of which they dipped their hot water when you needed to wash up. Some of the best cooking I have ever eaten came from that old stove. Her fried chicken and berry pies were out of this world. My mouth still waters when I think about her meals. It was country cookin' at its best! When she ironed clothes, she had to heat the flat irons on the stove. It was so cozy to gather around that old, black stove on a cold morning while she was cooking.

Of course they had an outdoor privy, complete with the half moon shape cutout over the door. It was a 2-holer, which meant you could have a companion while doing your business if you were so inclined. On a cold, frosty morning, one had to think long and hard before making the decision to go out there and plop your bottom on that wooden seat. The odor in those little houses was commonly horrific so you didn't want to sit there and meditate too long. Some folks would keep a bag of lime with an empty tin can to scoop a little out from time to time to pour down the holes to kill the odor. I never observed that it worked very well. There was often a mail order catalog to read or you could tear out pages to use for wiping.

In the wintertime, some folks kept what we called a chamber pot by the bed, and if you were rich, you might have a piece of furniture called a commode with a door on the front to hide the pot. There was a place on the top to hold a washbasin so you could wash up after doing your business in the pot, very convenient. The pots usually had a painting of a vase filled with beautiful flowers on the side. Maybe those flowers were there to draw your attention away from the odor coming from inside after its use.

Then there was the chore of emptying the chamber pot of a morning and washing it out in preparation for the next use. It beat that cold privy seat, though, by a mile, especially for the ladies. It was especially convenient for them if they could get their mate to empty the pot for them. That would be a demonstration of true love, often reserved for newly weds.

I once saw a poem framed and posted in a public out-house:

> *"This little throne,*
> *we call our own,*
> *we try to keep it neat.*
> *So please be kind*
> *with your behind,*
> *don't dirty on the seat!"*

I really got a chuckle out of that poem.

At the edge of the barnyard, there was a windmill with a long pipe leading to the watering tank for the livestock. When I was there, it was my assignment to pump water for the horses, cows and sheep when there was not enough wind to work the pump. That windmill fascinated my young mind and I studied and studied it. One day I decided to climb up and see what the mechanism looked like that converted the circular motion to a reciprocating motion needed to activate the pump. I climbed all the way up to the small platform just beneath the blades. It seemed like I could see for miles but all I could see were hills and more hills. I got a good scolding for climbing up there, but I discovered how it worked and I was satisfied.

Uncle Harry and Aunt Mae had a teenage son who lived on the farm with them. Everyone just called him "Junior," and Jody and I adored him. He spent a lot of time with us and loved to tease us. He told us really scary ghost stories, then later on of an evening, he would put a sheet over himself and jump out at us when were least expecting it. Sometimes I was so frightened that I could feel my hair standing on end. What great fun for a kid!

I don't think he was quite old enough to drive, but sometimes he would get us in their 1934 Ford in the side yard of the house. He would start it up and pop the clutch. That made it lurch and he would tell us there was a ghost under the car that made it jump.

Sometimes we would all be visiting at JC's house in Leipsic. Junior showed us all the nooks and crannies in that big, old house and each one had a story. He had us believing there were secret passageways that the ghosts used to make their way around in the house. He was very convincing with his stories that really appealed to our vivid imaginations.

There was a vacant room upstairs with a big hole in the ceiling where firemen had chopped an access to the attic to put out a small fire in the flue. He told us all kinds of stories about that hole and I would look at it and shudder to think of what creature might come down through it. There was a big mound of canned goods on the floor of that room, probably excess inventory from the store. We would sit there and eat Vienna sausages and throw the cans up through the hole. I imagine those cans are still up in the attic. It would be fun to give it a look-see. When I see Vienna sausages on the store shelf, I still think about eating them in my great grandfather's house. Funny, how memories stay with you.

Uncle Harry still farmed some with draft horses, although there was an iron-wheeled tractor in one of the sheds. He sometimes let me help harness the horses, and I felt I was essential to the project. He was really good with kids and had a lot of patience with us.

Snakes Alive

I can never remember being afraid of snakes and even played with garden snakes when I was just a little tyke. I guess Dad had showed me they were harmless. I would even put them in my toy trucks and give them rides. They seemed like they really enjoyed it. I had to be very careful not to ever let one loose in the house lest Mom skin me alive.

I was roaming around Uncle Harry's farm one day and saw a big, good-looking snake. I caught it and played with it for a while but didn't have a place to keep it. The 34 Ford was out in the yard so I stuck it in the glove compartment temporarily, while I went looking for a suitable container. To my horror, Aunt Mae came out of the house and jumped in the car to go to town. All I could do was watch.

She made it all the way down their long lane and had just turned onto the gravel road when the car slid to a stop in a cloud of dust. She jumped out and left the door open. It seemed that a snake had slithered out from beneath the seat just to say howdy. I didn't know he would get out of the glove box.

Amazingly, everyone seemed to assume that I had something to do with that snake being in the car. I never confessed to the deed, but I got a spanking without a fair trial. See, garden snakes *can* harm you!

Cut to the Chase

One day, I was out fooling around in the barnyard when I saw this big ram looking at me. I didn't think much about it and went on with my business of fooling around. Pretty soon, I noticed him again and we made eye contact. I guess he just didn't like my looks or maybe it was something I was wearing. Who knows? Anyway, that ole ram started to come after me.

I wasn't too worried because I thought I was a fast runner. At least I could outrun most of my friends at school. I also thought he would chicken out before he actually butted me. When he got pretty close, I was the one that chickened out and took off running. He surprised me how fast he could run and I was running flat out just to keep my distance. He might have been gaining on me a little.

I started to run around the barn to try to lose him but it was no use. I thought I would have better traction than him on the turns but such was not the case. That ole ram was sure determined to give me a good butting.

Well, around and around the barn we went and I was getting tired. I happened to notice that Jody, Mom and Aunt Mae were standing behind a wooden walk gate that separated the barnyard from the house. They were watching the whole thing with the attention one usually pays to a NASCAR race. I yelled to them to open the gate on the next lap.

They had it open when I ran by again and I sailed through. They closed it quickly and that ole ram hit it with a loud bang. I'll bet he was disappointed to be cheated out of a good butting. I ran into the house and locked the door behind me. I got teased a lot about that from then on. They would ask me if I was running as fast as I could and I would reply, "Naw, I never got it out of second gear." My answer would always elicit a hardy laugh.

That happened over 60 years ago, and I know there are still some folks around there who would tease me about it if they saw me.

Those visits to Southern Indiana were so wonderful that we always hated to go back to our "boring" life in Paris.

Chapter 3

War Comes to Our Town

PEARL HARBOR
DECEMBER 7, 1941, A DATE
WHICH WILL LIVE IN INFAMY...
NO MATTER HOW LONG IT
MAY TAKE US TO OVERCOME
THIS PREMEDITATED INVASION,
THE AMERICAN PEOPLE, IN
THEIR RIGHTEOUS MIGHT,
WILL WIN THROUGH
TO ABSOLUTE VICTORY.

> Words inscribed on the WW II Memorial, 2004
> From President Roosevelt's speech

Did you notice that the last phrase, *"SO HELP US GOD"* is left out of the inscription on the World War II memorial? It was in the president's speech!

I remember his Pearl Harbor speech on December 8, 1941, which came over the radio with a lot of screeches and static in the background. That day truly did live in infamy and changed the world forever.

On Sunday, December 7, 1941 our family left early for Galesburg, Illinois to visit Dad's sister, Ruby, and her family. Our 1937 Chrysler didn't have a radio so we knew nothing about the attack on Pearl Harbor until we arrived home late that evening. My grandfather, Me Mason, was staying at our house and met us at the door. He was very excited when he told us all the news about the Japanese attack. He had been listening to the radio all day. It was one of those happenings that make you remember exactly where you were and what you were doing when you heard the news. I was only in the first grade but I remember it vividly.

It was difficult to fathom how deeply the war would touch all of our lives.

Even before President Roosevelt declared war, it was raging in Europe. Hitler's army was conquering one country after another and he had his evil mind set on taking over the world. I came in the house one day and Dad was packing up one of his rifles. Of course, I was curious and asked him where he was sending it. He replied that it was going to Great Britain and I asked him why he was sending a perfectly good gun over there.

"Well," he said, "Those folks are going to be fighting the Nazis on their door steps and they don't have enough guns. All they have are clubs and pitch forks." He said that someday I would understand. This program was named the *Lend Lease Program* and tons of various kinds of military equipment were sent to England. You never hear much about that now. Sadly, most of those guns were melted down when the Brits enacted strict gun control laws a few years ago. The philosopher, George Santayana once said, "Those who cannot learn from history are doomed to repeat it." I understand it now, Dad.

Well, there we were in 1941 going to war on two fronts when we were not really prepared for any conflict. Many so-called experts predicted failure and thought we would eventually be speaking Japanese or German. They grossly underestimated the American people.

Tool Up & Turn To

This country came together like you wouldn't believe! Almost overnight, automobile manufacturers began making jeeps, tanks, and airplanes. The only 1942 model cars that were sold were already on the assembly lines or in dealers' inventories. Even cash register manufacturers were making guns; and, of course, the arms manufacturers were running full bore to turn out military weapons.

Stay at home moms were going off to work in defense plants and "Rosie the Riveter" became part of our culture. Guys were enlisting in droves and those who were fit were being drafted if they didn't enlist fast enough. Dad saw most of his buddies go off to war, but his knees had been crushed in an accident while he was working at McCord's. He quit his job at the service station and went to work at a factory in Paris where he helped make bodies for army vehicles. He bought a bicycle to ride back and forth to work. It eventually became my bike, the only one I had as a kid.

In all the schoolyards in town, temporary fences were erected in big circles and the townsfolk would throw metal items over the fence to be recycled into military equipment. It was amazing to see what items were donated. Aluminum was the metal they really needed badly for planes and there were nearly new pots and pans in the piles. It was almost like a contest to see who was willing to throw in the best stuff.

School kids were even enlisted to go out in neighborhoods with their wagons, knock on doors and ask if they had anything to contribute to the war effort. The town folk warmly welcomed us and would sometimes give us a little treat and thanked us for helping with the war effort. Patriotism was the name of the game in those days.

We took big sacks and went around the countryside gathering milkweed pods. The silky fibers inside the pods could be used in making parachutes. Ladies could not get nylon hose anywhere, so some bought leg-painting kits to make it look like they were wearing nylons. The kits even came with a little darker shade in a small container with an artist brush so they could paint on seams. Seamless hose were yet to be invented.

Tighten The Belts

Rationing of consumer goods was put in place soon after the war started. You had to have coupons or tokens to buy any of the rationed products. The rationed items included gasoline, tires, shoes, sugar, etc. There was a flourishing black market, but you would be looked down upon if you patronized it. I always wondered where they got the stuff.

Mom always squirreled away a little from her grocery allowance all year to make sure us kids had a nice Christmas. When I was nine years old, I wanted a Red Rider Repeater BB gun so badly that it almost made me sick. It was all I could think about and I would even wake up at night and think about it. Mom wanted to get me one for Christmas that year, 1943, but items like that were hard to come by during the war.

Mom's father had just passed away on December 21 that year so caring for him near the end and taking care of his funeral arrangements had taken its toll on her Christmas shopping spirit and time.

She spent an entire day in Terre Haute going from store to

store looking for a Red Rider gun but they were not to be had. She didn't want to see little Danny disappointed so she redoubled her effort. Finally, she found a "Plain Jane" single shot BB gun so she bought it.

On Christmas morning I started to unwrap the long, skinny box just knowing a Red Rider gun would soon be in my ready and waiting hands. Out came the single shot and spoiled little Danny began to cry. Dad took me in the other room and I was sure I was going to get a licking. Instead, he just sat me down and gave me a lecture on marksmanship.

He said that a good way to learn to be a good shot was to start out with a single shot. That way, you had to make every shot count and didn't try to make throwing a lot of lead make up for poor skills. He was a champion shooter so I listened to what he said, the tears dried up and I began to like my single shot. He was a very wise father. I'll bet I shot that old gun a million times over the years. I wish I still had it.

I was bad news for rats and mice that ventured out into my line of fire. My favorite thing was to go to a corncrib on a farm where mice and rats were running everywhere. You had to be on guard that a varmint didn't run up your pant leg. That could result in more excitement than you were prepared for. Sometimes the farmer would pay me a penny or two bounty for each corn-eating rat or mouse I delivered to them. I had to be careful that the farm cats didn't come around and eat up my evidence.

The Stars Come Out

When a family had a son, daughter or father in the service, it was customary to hang a little banner with a blue star in the front window. There was more than one banner in the window if more than one family member was serving. When I walked to school each morning I took notice of which houses had banners. The blue stars were numerous, but once in awhile a blue star banner would be changed to a gold star banner. This meant that the service person had been killed in action. When I saw a star change I would get so sad and then I would get mad. I wanted to go fight the enemy myself.

Of course my friends and I played war, and we gathered up anything that could be made to resemble something military. We dug foxholes and trenches where we could, and the old blackberry patch behind Me Mason's garden became a favorite battleground. We became really good at playing dead when we got shot and some of the performances might even have merited an Oscar. War movies were the order of the day and parents had to get used to their kids playing war. A surplus store in Terre Haute received a supply of army helmet liners that looked exactly like the real helmets. Word of this spread around the Paris kids like wildfire. I was lucky enough to get one before they sold out and it became my prized possession. I think I even tried to sleep with it on. If you had one of those helmets and an olive drab guard belt with a canteen attached to it, you were really living.

Before the war, I had made friends with a boy who was about 10 years older that me, who lived on our street. I will call him "Bobby." He was an expert builder of model airplanes and I loved to go to his room and see all the models hanging from the ceiling. Building a model airplane took some doing in those days. There were no plastic models and they had to be made with balsa wood ribs and spars and covered with shrunken tissue, similar to how a real plane was built. He even had a model of a Piper Cub where you could reach in the window, move the control stick, and the ailerons and elevators would actually move like a real plane; that was very impressive. He taught me a lot about model airplane building. I piddled around with it some, never reaching the skill level of Bobby's.

When the war started, Bobby enlisted in the Army Air Force and, not surprisingly, entered pilot training. I made it a point to stop at his house once in awhile and get an update about his adventures from his mom. Of course, I was envious of him and wished I were old enough to do what he was doing.

One day I was riding my bike by his house when his mom came out and flagged me down. She invited me into the house and then started to cry. A couple of days before, they had received word that Bobby's plane had been shot down and he was killed. I was shocked and saddened and didn't know what to say. She finally got her composure back and told me to go to Bobby's room and pick out a model to take home because Bobby would want me to have one of his planes. When I left her house with the plane, I cried when I noticed the gold star in the window. I kept the model for a while and enjoyed looking at it and thinking of Bobby. Sadly to say, I finally tore it up trying to fly it with its rubber band powered motor. I wish I still had it.

Speaking of airplanes, sometimes we would hear a distant drone that slowly became louder until it demanded our attention. When we looked up, the sky would be filled with airplanes. There would be fighters, B-25s, P-38s and a lot of B-17s, the famed Flying For- tresses. I got very excited when I saw those. Those four big en- gines had a special drone of their own. I couldn't identify some of the planes, but from somewhere, probably from sending in box tops, I had gotten an identification chart and I became the neighborhood authority on US aircraft. Sometimes these flyovers took place at night and that was kind of scary because you couldn't help wondering if they were ours. When I ran outside and looked up, the sky would be so full that the black silhouettes almost blot- ted out the moon.

I believe the reason for all these planes flying over was that Paris was not far from Chanute Field, a big Army Air Force base, and we hap- pened to be in the flight pattern.

Dad's war effort, besides working in the defense industry, was teaching the guys who were about to go to war how to shoot. The men in the Paris Rifle Club kind of had a team to do the training. It was so necessary to get the new soldiers into battle as soon as possible that they were rushed through basic training and never really received extensive marksmanship instruction. The guys in the club tried to remedy this shortcoming. When the war was over, the club received a citation from the US government for their service to the soldiers.

Dad's friends, who left for the service, were highly motivated to go and defend their homeland. There was no thought of going somewhere to escape the draft. In fact, if someone had even mentioned it, he would probably have had a fight on his hands

Dad had a good friend named Tommy who went through the club's training program and then fought in Europe after his boot camp training. I think he fought with General Patton and was in the thick of combat. Once in a while Dad got a letter from him. Dad had taken special pains with him to train him how to be a good shot with a pistol. In one letter, he told how he had surprised a German officer and the officer jumped up and started wildly shooting at Tommy with his Luger pistol. Tommy leveled his .45 and took him out with one shot. He credited Dad with saving his life by teaching him how to shoot straight. I don't know what ever happened to that letter. Dad kept it for a long time. Sadly, Tommy went missing in action and was never heard from again.

Blacken Those Windows

Sometimes you heard the sound of a siren and that meant we were having an air raid drill, hopefully just a drill. You were supposed to take cover in the safest place you could find. If your house had a basement, you were supposed to be down there. There were civil defense volunteers that would come around and check on your compliance. We used to make fun of their little flat metal hats.

Sometimes these drills were held at night and you were supposed to turn off all the lights or have blinds on the windows that would not let any light out. If a civil defense guy checked your house and saw any light, he knocked on your door and told you to blacken those windows or turn off your light. Cars on the street were supposed to come to a stop with their lights turned off. They wanted the cities to be invisible from the air.

When the siren sounded again, it meant that the drill was over. This kind of stuff could be really scary for little kids. We bigger kids liked the excitement and listened for bombs to drop. Thank God they never did!

Wild Teeth

When I was in the second grade or so, I noticed that a new tooth was coming in that was way out of line with my other teeth. I was too scared to tell anyone and I kept feeling it with my tongue, which made the tip of my tongue sore. It got bigger and bigger and I knew that I should tell someone. One day, Mom was ironing in the living room and we were talking about things in general. I finally got my nerve up and told her about the tooth. She looked at it, felt it with her finger and looked very concerned.

I don't know if she told Dad but nothing happened, except that my mind was relieved that I had told someone. A while later, another tooth poked through in a weird place. Then I was really worried that my mouth would look like a jungle. I gave this information to Mom and Dad, which prompted a trip to the family dentist, Dr. S. He was a very good dentist but when he had his stomach next to your ear while he examined you, it would growl. I swear that on one occasion it clearly said, "Hello." It was common knowledge that his gut made funny

35

noises, and the kids in town exchanged stories about what it said to them.

Dr. S. kept shaking his head while he examined me. Mom was standing there with that concerned look on her face. When he was finished, he turned to Mom and said, "This boy needs to see an orthodontist." I didn't even know what an orthodontist was. He recommended Dr. Welch in Terre Haute and said that he was about the best there was in that area. He called Dr. Welch and made an appointment for an examination.

Mom and I made the trip to Terre Haute where Dr. Welch's office was on the eighth floor in a building at the corner of Wabash Avenue and another street. I thought the elevator would never stop going up as the numbers flipped by. I had never been this high in a building before.

When I met Dr. Welch, I liked him instantly. He and his nurse really had a way with kids and laid my fears to rest. When he examined me, he shook his head just the way that Dr. S. had shaken his. When he was finished, he turned to Mom and said that I was about the worst case he had ever seen. He said that he could move teeth around but that I had one so far out of place he was not sure he could stretch the nerve that far. I'm sure this was welcome news to my mother. Always good news to find out your kid needs braces.

Mom asked if there were any alternatives like pulling all the new teeth and replacing them with a partial plate. He said that it could be done but it would result in me having a severely receding chin. Our family had a very modest income so it was a tough decision to make. Eventually, the decision was made for their Danny to get braces. I had seen only rich kids wear braces so I thought it might be fun to impress everyone with mine. I had a lot to learn about orthodontic work.

Thus began a series of weekly trips to Terre Haute to see Dr.

Welch. My parents had to go before the rationing board to get an extra gas allotment to make the frequent trips. Oftentimes, Dr. Welch would have another orthodontist look in my mouth while he pointed out certain aspects of my condition. There was usually the head shaking that I was familiar with. One time he had a conference with about four other experts and they all looked in my mouth and shook their heads. It seemed the act of head shaking was required if you looked at my teeth. One of the men was from another country and I couldn't understand what he was saying since he spoke in broken English. He seemed to be the authority in the group because they all seemed to hang on his every word. But, maybe he talked so funny that they had to strain to understand what he was saying. It all made me feel rather famous and I got to thinking maybe I should charge admission if anyone wanted to look in my mouth.

After about three years, the result was that the project was successful and I ended up with a beautiful set of teeth. It was a struggle wearing braces and keeping new rubber bands in place for three long years, but I thought Dr. Welch was a wizard.

The downside was that it cost my parents a bundle of money and they had to delay the purchase of the new car they had been saving for. I think my dental work cost around $600.00, which was a lot of money in those days. They lived in fear that I would get some teeth knocked out since I liked to play rough games.

Once when Dad and I were hunting, we were sitting under a tree when Dad told me how much the cost was, and that they still had to drive the old 37 Chrysler for a while longer. I guess he was just trying to make me realize what they sacrificed for my teeth, but I'm not sure it really soaked through my skull until years later. When I reached adulthood, I thanked them for their sacrifice. They eventually did get a new car but it was a few years later. Meanwhile, I had to learn to drive in the old car.

Little Treats

Understandably, special treats were few and far between during the war. We had to be content with little things. Mom loved what she called Eskimo Pies, which were chocolate covered ice cream chunks on a stick. Carli's, on Vance Street, was a neighborhood store that specialized in fun stuff for kids and I loved to go there. They used to have little wax bottles filled with Kool-aid and you bit the top off to drink the liquid inside. Sometimes they had them in the shape of a pistol and I especially liked those.

About once a week or so, Mom would gather her change together and send me to the store on my bike to bring us back Eskimo Pies. I think they only cost a nickel each, but a nickel then was probably worth something like a dollar now. I had to rush home with the treats before they melted. If I saw a friend on the way home, I had to excuse myself and get on home before the ice cream melted. One time I saw a girl I liked and let her have mine, talked to her a little while and lost Mom's portion of the cargo. I felt silly taking her a bare stick inside an ice cream soaked sack. However, I think she understood.

My grandfather, Me Mason, loved to take car rides. That was about his only outing when his wife was bedridden with cancer. His rides were limited after gas rationing took place during the war. By that time he was a widower and really enjoyed the times with his family. So, the folks skimped on rationed gas in order to take him on car rides once in awhile.

Dad drove, and my grandfather always sat in the front seat of the Chrysler. Mom, Jody and I would sit in the back, kind of crowded. Me Mason chewed tobacco but Dad hated for him to chew in the car. Well, he would get to craving it and would pull out a plug and poke it in his mouth. Of course, he had to spit once in a while so would just let it fly out the window. Unbeknownst to him, if we were on the highway with the back windows rolled down, a large portion of the juice whipped right in the back window and our clothes would be covered with brown polka dots when the ride was over. What a treat, to get a load of tobacco juice right in the kisser all of a sudden. We got to where we tried to anticipate his spitting and quickly rolled the window up. He was such a sweet man that no one wanted to offend him by telling him his chewing was obnoxious.

Another nice diversion from wartime concerns was fishing. Dad had an old wooden boat that usually required maintenance every winter that he would perform in our big garage by the heat of an old pot bellied stove. I helped with this project even when I was just a little guy. There was always scraping caulk out of seams, then re-caulking and painting to be done. One year he had to replace one whole side, which was a major operation.

When he took me fishing out on Twin Lakes I was in heaven. We could depend on catching crappies and blue gills early in the spring, and then bass all summer. He trained me to row the boat along the bank at a distance of about 100 feet while he cast for bass. I became quite proficient at rowing a boat.

Sometimes I would sit on his metal tackle box in the bottom of the boat close to him and he would tell me stories. Many of the stories were about how the war was going, and sometimes they were not very encouraging. They became sad when he told about a particular friend who had been killed. I have that old tackle box and open it up now and then. Every lure evokes a memory or two and I treasure it. I wrote a note about it and left it inside so that those who have it after me will know the history of it.

He always insisted on tying a rope around my ankle with the other end tied to one of the oarlocks. We didn't have life jackets so he thought if I fell in, he could just pull me into the boat with the rope. I was ashamed of that rope but I never could talk him out of using it. When we would pull alongside another boat to swap fish stories with the occupant, I would always try to hide the rope.

When I was in the fifth grade, the teacher had a class picnic for us at Twin Lakes Park. In those days, the park had a dancing pavilion with a jukebox, an arcade and a snack shop. There was a small marina near the swimming beach where one could dock a boat and they also had rowboats and paddleboats for rent. In the ride area, there was a merry-go-round, and an airplane and little car rides for younger kids. There were picnic tables scattered all around.

Then there was a giant, motorized swing with the swings hanging down on chains from the big circular top. You would get in a seat, strap yourself in, and the swings would start going in a big circle. It would go faster and faster until the centrifugal force caused the riders to swing out at an angle of at least 45 degrees. It was pretty wild and the younger kids weren't allowed to ride on it. When one of the riders would get sick, they sure made it miserable for the nearby bystanders and picnickers. That park was a very neat place and folks came from miles around to enjoy it.

Back to the fifth grade picnic: I got a couple of girls to go with me to the boat dock where Dad's boat was moored. Promise a girl a rowboat ride and they will follow you anywhere. We got in the boat and I started to row them around the lake. I was in complete control and I thought I was Mr. Cool. When we passed the picnic site, I glanced over to see how many people I was impressing. I saw my teacher there on the edge of the lake waving her arms and yelling something. Her face was all red and I thought she was having a fit. She was having a fit all right! Well, I kind of got the message that I should end the little boat outing so we went back to the dock where the teacher was waiting. She was more than a little upset and I was on her goofball list big time. I was happy that school was almost out for the summer.

We could always find ways to have fun, even when times were

hard and the war was raging.

Diseases

When I was in the fourth grade, I came down with scarlet fever. In those days, you had to be quarantined for a month. They placed a sign on our door so that no one would enter. Mom and I stayed in our house while Dad and Jody stayed with Dad's folks. Every evening, they would come and stand in the alley while Mom and I stood at Jody's window overlooking the alley. It was probably illegal but we had some nice visits. Our groceries had to be placed on the front porch to avoid any chance of contact with the dreaded disease.

While Mom and I were stranded at home, she read books to me. She read about Tom Sawyer, Huck Finn and Robin Hood, among others. I was so touched by the Robin Hood story that for a long time I pretended to be him. I didn't rob any rich people, but I practiced with my bow and got pretty good with it.

I came through with no complications, which was a blessing and, since I had enjoyed all the attention, I kind of hated to have it end. I now treasure that time I spent one-on-one with my mother.

Not long after that, I came down with the mumps and my parents were afraid it would "go down" on me so they wouldn't let me jump around much. I guess that can make you sterile, but Twila and I have four children so it turned out not to be a problem.

Mom lived in fear of polio; I guess because Dad's sister Ruby's son, Bobby had it and had to wear a brace on his leg from then on. I was not allowed to swim in Twin Lakes after the fourth of July each year because they thought you could catch it from stagnant water. There were a lot of theories going around, and whenever a new one came out, you had to avoid some new activity. It kind of cramped my style.

Welcome Little Stranger

On June 2, 1944, my little brother, Gary, was born. It was just 4 days before D-Day. By this time, Dad had changed jobs and worked the night shift at the Railway Express Company in Paris. This job was also essential for national defense, as they had to handle lots of military parts being shipped across the country to defense plants. It was a real challenge for him to unload an airplane wing from a freight car onto his cart and then load it back onto another train all by himself. Needless to say, he was very tired when he came home of a morning and could only think about sleeping.

Well, Gary would sometimes get a little fussy and that really complicated things when Dad tried to sleep during the day. Jody and I needed to get him out of the house while Dad was trying to sleep. We put him in the stroller and he quieted down the minute he sat down. We then took turns pushing him for hours it seemed. All over the streets of Paris we pushed him, mile after mile. I'll bet we pushed that old stroller 10,000 miles. I can still remember the left front wheel shimmying when we got up a little speed. Jody and I contributed quite a bit to the rearing of Gary.

Gary wouldn't stay in his crib and would climb out over the side. You would put him to bed and say goodnight and go into the living room, and sometimes he would beat you there. It was a rather hopeless situation. Put him in, he'd climb out, put him in, he'd climb out, time after time. Dad finally made a top for the crib, which could be tied down with a cord on each corner. That did the trick, and he had to stay put in his cage. But he got used to it and would go right to sleep. Relief at last! Parents would probably get into trouble with the authorities if they did that now.

In spite of Jody's and my influence, Gary grew up to be a fine, Christian man. He and his wife, Judy, have a wonderful family of two sons and one daughter, all married with children. The time I spent taking care of him when he was little, paid off, for I now have a great brother!

Basketball Madness

During the 1940s, Paris High School had one of the very best basketball teams in the state of Illinois. Ernie Eveland was the coach. It is reported that during his career, his teams won a total of 779 games. They won 30 games or more for six seasons in a row. During a 12-year span they won two state championships, two second places and a third place. Back then, the schools were not divided into divisions; therefore, little Paris had to go up against the huge schools in Chicago as well as other large schools such as Decatur and Champaign. When one considers this, their accomplishments are even more impressive.

Coach Eveland was so intense during games that folks in town used to joke about him wearing out the seat of his pants every game because he was jumping up off the bench so often. The intensity, discipline and hard work by him and his team was what won games.

As you can imagine, the whole town was crazy about high school basketball. However, there was some polarization. Some folks thought that Coach's tactics were just too intense for players at the high school level. This became a popular subject for discussion, even heated arguments, amongst the barbershop crowd.

My Uncle Jack was on Eveland's team at the forward position during his playing days. Jack was the kid brother of my dad and was my idol. He was just a baby when Mom and Dad were married in 1928. He could do little wrong in my eyes, and you can imagine what level of heaven I dwelled in when he occasionally played ball with me out beside his house on North Street. I was the envy of my friends. Those were the days of two-handed set shots and underhand free throws, but they were effective for the times.

I pleaded with Dad to put up a basketball hoop on the front of our garage and he finally did so to get me off his case. The court in front of the hoop was just a rough, crushed rock driveway that provided a challenge for dribbling. I also had to be careful that a rebound didn't go over the gooseberry hedge where Mrs. Fisk might confiscate it. My friends often rode their bikes over and we spent many happy hours out in front of that garage shooting baskets, going one-on-one and playing h-o-r-s-e. I had to continue cautioning them about not letting a ball go over the hedge to become Mrs. Fisk's ball.

Basketball provided a much needed diversion from the war that was raging in Europe and the Pacific.

The War Ends

In August, 1945, the bombs were dropped on the two Japanese cities. There is a lot of controversy about that these days, some 60 plus years after the fact. The fact is that it saved lots of lives. We were getting prepared to invade the Japanese mainland, which would have been the bloodiest of all battles, much worse than the Normandy Invasion. Most folks, at the time, agreed with President Truman's decision to use the ultimate weapon.

I remember going to church at the First Baptist Church in Paris the Sunday after the first bomb was dropped on Hiroshima. There was my Uncle Bill, who had a PhD in chemistry, surrounded by a bunch of guys who were listening to him tell how an atomic bomb worked. He really sounded like he knew what he was talking about. I was very impressed and proud that he was my uncle.

Just days after the second bomb was dropped, Japan surrendered at a ceremony held on the deck of the battleship *USS Missouri* anchored in Tokyo Bay. In 1955, my wife, Twila, and I visited the *USS Missouri* in mothballs in Bremerton, Washington and stood next to the brass plate on the deck that commemorates the signing of the unconditional surrender papers at that very spot. That was a touching experience for me.

Hitler had committed suicide earlier that year and the German army surrendered. Thus ended World War II without a whimper. The greatest war of all time was over. It was hard to take it all in.

Well, it was celebration time for a while. Then the "Greatest Generation" went to work and the post war recovery and baby boom began. The rest, as they say, is history.

Warriors I Have Known

In the 1960s, I worked for a large utility company in Indiana. Our company photographer was a young man from Germany whose name has slipped my mind. He was the finest photographer I have ever known, before or since. He could do magic with a camera before the days of computer photograph enhancement.

We were having coffee one morning in the company break room when he told about some of his experiences in WW II. We perked up our ears when he said that he fought in North Africa with German Field Marshall General Erwin Rommel, the famed "Desert Fox."

He told us that he was the commander of a Panzer IV tank, which was a wonderfully built machine. It has the distinction of being the only tank to remain in continuous production throughout the war.

Then he started to compare the Panzer with the American tanks of the line, which he came up against in his battles. He said that there was no comparison, the Sherman tanks being a pile of junk next to the German Panzers. He said that they laughed when they saw them and heard them rattling along. That statement really irked his listeners, but he went on: *"But,"* he said, *"*You had so damn many of 'em!"

He was right about that. The US produced over 50,000 medium frame, M4 Sherman tanks for use by the US forces and our allies during WW II.

He built a 40-foot sailboat in a shed in Northern Indiana and sailed it through the great lakes, the St. Lawrence Seaway and across the Atlantic to Germany. It took him about three years to build it out of oak strips and it exhibited unbelievable workmanship.

One of my friends, Jack Gambrell, fought with General Patton in Europe. He saw combat action in the Battle of the Bulge, the last major offensive by the Nazi army, which was begun December 16, 1944 in the Ardennes Forest in an attempt by the German infantry to break through the allied line. The attempt was a failure but many troops were lost in that hard fought battle.

The last time I visited with Jack, he told me that he was riding in a troop carrier, with just a few GIs, through a dense part of the forest, when, all at once, about 200 German soldiers came out of the brush and stepped onto the dirt road ahead of them. He thought, "Well, this is it for us." But, to his surprise, the German soldiers all threw down their weapons and surrendered. "Then," he said, "We were faced with the problem of what to do with all those prisoners."

Sadly, Mr. Gambrell passed away as I was working on this book. We are losing so many WW II veterans now. I have heard the numbers estimated at around 1,000 per day but I would put it higher than that. They deserve our honor and respect because they preserved our freedom and rebuilt our great nation.

I recently visited an old friend, Mel Crawford. He was an airborne radar technician in the Navy during WW II, and was privileged to work on some legendary aircraft such as the PBY Flying Boat and the F4U, the beautiful, gull-wing Corsair, the fastest plane in the Navy at that time. The Japanese called it "Whistling Death" because of the sound it made when diving for a strike. During the Korean War, pilots of Corsairs could even shoot down MIG 15s.

Mel was stationed at the strategic Henderson Field on Guadalcanal, which had been the center of fierce fighting between the US Marines and the Japanese soldiers as the Japanese tried to retake the air strip but failed. When Mel was there, there were still a few Japanese soldiers left stranded on the island. He said they were pretty pathetic and sometimes visited the GIs where they were given food from time to time.

Mel said that one of their worst enemies was the mosquito. One night, two of them were flying around in the barracks when they were overheard discussing one of the sleeping sailors: the first mosquito asked, "Shall we eat him here or take him home?" The second one replied, "Let's eat him here because if we take him home, our big brothers will just take him away from us!" Now those were mighty big mosquitoes!

I asked Mel about bravery and what makes one man fight while another one turns and runs away? He replied that he thought it was all in how you were brought up and whether you were taught to accept responsibility or flee from it. I thought it was a good answer. I have heard others say that a brave person is just as afraid as a coward but is willing to fight in spite of fear.

When he returned home from the service, he asked a girl he knew to marry him and they were married nine days later. He worked for the Underwood Typewriter Company as a technician and eventually owned his own successful business machine company in Austin, Texas. He and his beloved Jean, enjoyed a long, happy marriage and raised two fine sons. Jean went to be with the Lord a few years ago but Mel has many happy memories of their life together.

Mr. Crawford truly is a member in good standing of The Greatest Generation!

Chapter 4

Peace Returns

"And he shall judge among the nations,
and shall rebuke many people:
and they shall beat their swords into plowshares,
and their spears into pruning hooks:
nation shall not lift up sword against nation,
neither shall they learn war any more."

Isaiah 2:4 (KJV)

Although the above prophecy is not believed to apply to this time in history, it seemed appropriate to quote those lines at the beginning of this chapter.

World War II ended on August 15, 1945 and we celebrate it as V-J Day, the victory over Japan. As stated before, Germany had already surrendered.

All in all, government records show that there were over 360,000 American servicemen killed; in addition, almost 79,000 are still unaccounted for. Many were buried in unmarked graves because they could not be identified. The memorial in Arlington National Cemetery commemorates the unknown soldiers. What a price to pay for freedom! Let's not forget these and other sacrifices made so that we can live free. The following words are engraved on the monument:

"Here Rests
In Honored Glory
An American Soldier
Known But To God"

The WORLD WAR II memorial was built in Washington DC in 2004 and it was long overdue. Twila's brother, Ken Bridwell, a Navy veteran, who saw action as a medic aboard an LST during the Normandy invasion, was able to visit the memorial just days after the dedication. I'm sure it was an emotional experience for him.

Getting Back to "Normal"

In his book, *The Greatest Generation*, Tom Brokaw describes the men and women who fought WW II as those who weathered the great depression, learned to make do, and then went to war and won great victories. Everyone was making the same sacrifices so they were just part of a dedicated team that was determined to win. They came back from the Great War and rebuilt the nation. Although America won the war, the nation had taken a beating from the war effort and needed retooling and a new beginning.

I observed the rebuilding from the perspective of an eleven-year-old boy and it was amazing, even in our small town. The shortage of critical goods that had been rationed slowly came to an end, and it was wonderful to be able to buy things again. As the factories retooled, new cars, while still scarce, slowly began appearing on the streets and it was an event to spot one. Eventually, you could once again buy enough gasoline to take road trips.

New subdivisions were springing up since the returning GIs

could get VA loans with a low down payment and low interest rates. Some of them wanted to continue their education and colleges were hard pressed to handle the surge. In many cases, the colleges had to erect temporary buildings for veteran housing and classes.

In a few months, babies started coming right and left and the great American baby boom began.

More young men could be seen on the streets and, sadly, some were crippled from injuries in the war. They were treated well, though, and even revered by those who were able to keep the home fires burning while they were away.

My wife, Twila, had two brothers, Vic and Ken Bridwell who were good examples of the greatest generation. When they returned from the Navy, they started a tiny grocery store on the west side of Paris. When they got it all stocked and opened the door for business, they had $100.00 in change to put in the cash register for the first day. That was all the money they had between them.

Their little store did a thriving business and they eventually owned and operated one of the largest and most popular super markets in town.

Boy Scouts

I suppose I had admired the soldiers so much that I wanted to wear a uniform too. When I was eleven, I was old enough to join a boy scout troop that met in the basement of the Methodist Church on North Central Avenue and I would ride my bike over there every Monday evening to attend the troop meetings. I was really proud to march in parades in uniform since there were usually members of the American Legion marching in the same parade with us. Those were the guys I had such great admiration for.

Ross Wright was the scoutmaster and he had his hands full. We were a lively bunch of restless boys. I don't remember that he had much adult help except to drive us to campsites. A weekend of camping with these young hellions was no doubt taxing for him, but he handled it well.

We were camping once, when a potato was crammed into Mr. Wright's tail pipe on his old Chevy by some mischievous boy. I won't mention any names. When he started his car to run an errand, the potato flew out like a bullet and took down a tent that was in the line of fire. That is just an example of some of the tricks that were played on poor Mr. Wright.

When summer camp time rolled around, the troop planned to go for a week at Camp Krietenstein over in Indiana, east of Terre Haute. My parents had never had to make a decision like this before. Sending their little Danny away for a whole week was unthinkable. At first Dad said no, but I kept pleading and bugging him about it. He finally asked to talk to Mr. Wright. He came over to our house one evening and he and Dad hit it off pretty well, so I was given permission to go. But, as I remember, I had to come up with half the cost myself.

I somehow managed to save enough money to go and I had a wonderful time there. We stayed in bunkhouses and there was a lot of swimming, learning Indian lore, mastering scout skills like building a signal tower, etc.

My scouting career was somewhat successful as I attained the rank of Second Class. I almost made First Class but couldn't pass the life saving merit badge, which was required.

When I was an adult, I was a scoutmaster for six years and experienced some of the same things that Mr. Wright had endured so many years before.

I still remember the scout oath and law:

SCOUT OATH
On my honor
I will do my best
to do my duty
to God and my country,
and to obey the Scout Law,
to help other people
at all times,
to keep myself
physically strong,
mentally awake,
and morally straight.

SCOUT LAW
A scout is:
Trustworthy
Loyal
Helpful
Friendly
Courteous
Kind
Obedient
Cheerful
Thrifty
Brave
Clean
Reverent

Over the years, I have tried to use the oath and law as a sort of code of behavior. I regret that I have not always lived up to that standard. Thankfully, we have a forgiving Savior!

Off to Wrigley Field

When I was in sixth grade, I got to wear a white guard belt and help younger kids across the streets around Vance School. Near the end of the school year, the Paris Jaycees decided to give the patrol boys a nice outing. They decided to scrape enough gas and tires together for their pre-war cars to take us to a baseball game in Chicago. This was a major undertaking for the time because Chicago was about 150 miles to the North, and Wrigley Field was on the north side of Chicago.

We left early one Saturday morning and the caravan of cars lined up to take us was truly a sight to behold. One or two spare tires were tied to the tops of most of the cars and some had cans of gas tied on top of the rear bumpers. We kids didn't care if we looked like the Beverly Hillbillies; we were going to see the Cubs play Philadelphia. I remember climbing into a battered Plymouth with tattered seats and going down the road with a thump, thump, thump that rattled your teeth. There was a boot in a rear tire. We had to stop several times for a tire change on one or more of the cars. What fun it was for small boys, though. Could be that the men were having more fun than we were.

Wonder of all wonders, we stopped for lunch at Mickleberry's Log Cabin restaurant. None of us had ever been to a place as fancy as this. We were so impressed.

We saw the game but, for the life of me, I can't remember who won. The trip back to Paris was much like the trip going, but we made it home at a late hour. I don't remember where we stopped for supper. Weren't those Jaycee guys great to treat us to that outing?

Paper Route

When I was old enough, I began delivering newspapers for Paris

Beacon News. As I recall, I started when I was in sixth grade at Vance School and continued with it when I went to Mayo Junior High School. Every evening after school, my friend Floyd Rose and I would ride our bikes to the newspaper office to pick up the papers for our routes.

The newspaper office on North Main Street looks pretty much the same now as it did then, at least the street view does. When I am in Paris and drive by it, it brings back memories.

The printing press was an ancient looking machine and it was not unusual for it to break down, which would delay us picking up our stack of papers. The pressmen would scurry around frantically to fix it as soon as possible.

When we received our stack of papers, we took them over to the room where the delivery boys met. The walls were lined with bins that had shelves in front of them. We placed our stack of papers on the shelf and folded each one into a square, tucking the loose ends in so they would stay together when we threw them onto porches. It seems like I folded a million papers and I still remember how to do it.

As we folded the papers, we threw them into the bin. When they were all folded, we packed them tightly in our canvas bag with the words, "Paris Beacon News" stenciled on the front. The bags had a strap so they could be carried over the shoulder, but we wrapped the strap around the handlebars on our bikes so the papers would be in a convenient place just above the front wheel. We could easily reach for them while riding our bikes.

When the bags were all packed with papers and properly affixed to our handlebars, off we would go to run our route.

Those papers had to be delivered come rain or snow or sleet, and we had a code stricter than the postmen have. You need a lot of practice to attain the skill of riding by houses at full speed while sailing a folded newspaper accurately. I soon learned the law of physics that states that an object ejected from a moving platform will curve in the direction of travel. I learned to compensate for this effect and would need to let it go before I got abreast of the target porch. At first, I was a poor thrower and had to get off my bike often to pick up a paper that had missed.

Once I ripped a hole in a screen door and another time I actually broke a plate glass window. I then had to stop at the house and make arrangements to pay for the damage. It hurt so much to take the money out of my hard earned pay that I tried to keep this activity to a minimum. I always hated to see a cat or dog lounging on a porch because, no matter how I tried to avoid it, the paper would tend to curve toward it. It seemed like pets had a sort of magnetic attraction to papers. Sometimes a dog would like to have some fun by chasing me. They annoyed me but I never suffered from a bite, although some of the other carriers did. I just considered them to be another job hazard.

It was particularly miserable delivering papers when it was raining or snowing. I had an old piece of a raincoat I would put over my bag of papers to keep them dry. My customers hated wet newspapers, and some would not pay me for them. It was OK if I got wet, but not my papers!

Once there was a wet snow falling and it would tend to ball up on my tires and act as a brake when it got thick enough to rub the fenders. I stopped at a number of houses to borrow a pan of hot water to pour over my tires to melt the snow. At one spot, at a long distance between houses, my tires balled up and I didn't have access to any hot water. The snow was coming down thick and it made visibility so poor that I thought I could urinate on the tires without being seen. I tried it with mixed results but felt guilty about doing it. I only did it once, honestly. I made it home very late that evening and I was sure happy to get there.

I had my route down pat and I knew it like the back of my

hand. I learned every shortcut and would go down alleys, across backyards and even through a hedge, but not the gooseberry one, of course. One day, I was cutting across a yard when suddenly I found myself sprawled out on the ground with my papers scattered everywhere. It seemed the owner had put up a clothesline that day and a wire had caught me under the chin. Good thing I wasn't going faster or I might have been minus a head! As it was, I had a sore neck for several days and had trouble talking for a while. Four inches higher and the wire would have caught me right in my orthodontic mouth. There would have been heck to pay then!

Every Saturday I had to take my little receipt book and go collecting from my customers for the week's delivery. Many of the folks would be gone when I knocked on their door or saw who it was and avoided opening it. I loved it when they left the money under the mat for me. I had a personal policy that I would cut off their service after they missed three weeks of payment. I think some just wanted a free paper for a while and I thought that anyone who would cheat a paperboy was pretty low. I loved to collect just before Christmas because lots of the customers would give me a gift of money or candy or other things. One old lady gave me a big spider plant and I had a terrible time getting it home on my bike. Mom liked the plant and kept it for a long time.

I then took my collected money to the paper office and paid my weekly bill. I only made a few cents per paper but it added up. When a customer didn't pay, the carrier had to take the hit. They usually had our papers ready for us early on Saturdays and there was no Sunday edition.

I tried to get done early in the afternoon on Saturdays, and would meet Floyd Rose downtown at a theater where they showed double feature cowboy movies in the afternoon. There was always a serial episode shown between the films and they were fun. After the movie, we would discuss how we thought the cliffhanger would end. We would just *have* to go back the next Saturday, and the next, and the next. They also showed the weekly newsreel, which is mostly how we kept up with news about the war.

The theater was rather old and run-down, and Mom didn't like for me to go there because she was afraid I would get head lice. There would sometimes be bats flying around and the girls would all scream. Once a rat went running down the aisle with a cat right behind it. You never knew what you would see in that old theater, truly a fun place for a boy!

Post-War Economy (1946)

Dow Jones Industrial Average:	192.61
Average Household Net Worth:	$791.90
Average cost of new house:	$5,600.00
Average wages per year:	$2,500.00
Average cost of a new car:	$1,120.00
One gallon of gasoline:	15 cents
Bread, loaf:	11 cents
Cereal, 8 oz box:	11 cents
Chicken, lb:	41 cents
Coffee, 4 oz:	29 cents
Eggs, dozen:	64 cents
Lettuce, head:	11 cents
Soup, Campbell's tomato:	8 cents
Men's shirt:	$3.70
Men's shoes:	$1.89
Women's blouse:	$2.90
Women's sweater:	$4.98
Women's shoes:	$2.89
Couch, studio:	$39.97
Dining room set:	$30.75
High chair:	$7.98

Note that clothing was expensive in comparison to other consumer items. I suppose that is why most women of modest means chose to make clothing for themselves and members of their families. Mom used to spend hours at her treadle sewing machine just singing hymns and sewing away. She really seemed to enjoy it. She even utilized feed-sack cloth, which could be obtained with printed patterns, to make clothing for herself and Jody.

One year, Meme Hall made me three or four flannel shirts before school started in the fall. They were OK but I liked the store bought ones better. I remember that I had trouble keeping one of them buttoned. I wonder if I ever thanked her for making those shirts. I doubt it!

What We Heard

Here are the top 10 hits for 1946:

1) Ink Spots, "The Gypsy"
2) Frankie Carle, "Oh What it Seemed to Be"
3) Frankie Carle, "Rumors are Flying"
4) Dinah Shore, "The Gypsy"
5) Eddy Howard, "To Each His Own"
6) Frank Sinatra, "Oh What it Seemed to Be"
7) Sammy Kaye, "The Old Lamp-Lighter"
8) Nat King Cole, "For Sentimental Reasons"
9) Vaughn Monroe, "Let it Snow"
10) Perry Como, "Prisoner of Love"

What We Saw

Best movies of 1946 (Author's Opinion):

"It's a Wonderful Life" (5 Oscar Nominations)
James Stewart

"Beauty and the Beast"

"The Best Years of Our Lives"
Fredrick March
Virginia Mayo
Myrna Loy

"Duel in The Sun"
Gregory Peck
Jennifer Jones

"Courage of Lassie"
Elizabeth Taylor

Chapter 5

Out on the Illinois Prairie

*"It was planted in a good soil
by great waters, that it might
bring forth branches, and that it
might bear fruit, that it might be
a goodly vine."*
                    Ezekiel 17:8 (KJV)

*"For as the earth bringeth
forth her bud, and as the garden
causeth the things that are sown
in it to spring forth; so the Lord
God will cause righteousness and
praise to spring forth before all
the nations."*
                    Isaiah 61:11 (KJV)

When one leaves the City of Paris heading north, northwest, or west, and leaves the gently rolling hills, the land becomes almost as flat as a tabletop. The soil changes from gray-brown sandy clay to black loam. When a crow lands on freshly plowed earth, it is almost invisible. They say that one time a herd of Black Angus cattle strayed onto a freshly plowed field and disappeared for a week. You do you believe that story, don't you?

This area was once dotted with long hedgerows for the purpose of breaking the wind, which sometimes gets to whipping over this flat country, but these are rarely seen now. Those hedgerows provided wonderful cover for wild game and we liked to hunt pheasants along them when I was a kid. When they were removed, many predicted that the Illinois prairie could result in another dust bowl, but modern farming methods have now mostly mitigated this possibility.

This area is mostly planted in corn and soybeans now, and the soil is so fertile that it is not uncommon for corn production to top 200 bushels per acre and soybeans to top fifty bushels. Compare this with the sixty or so bushels of corn per acre back in the open pollination days. Plant research and development, along with modern farming methods, have produced wondrous results in crop yields.

When I was a kid, the farms also produced winter wheat and oats, with clover being planted about every four years to add nitrogen to the soil. The clover was harvested as hay to feed the dairy cows and other livestock. Dairy cattle are rarely seen in this area now.

These days, when you drive down a secondary country road, it is almost like driving in a tunnel with the tall corn stalks close to the road on each side, with the big ears hanging down. The corn grows as high as an "elephant's eye", which is an old country saying. They say that corn has to be at least knee high by the fourth of July to produce a good crop. That rule of thumb is somewhat outdated these days, since it is usually much taller than that in an average growing season.

A century or so ago, it was possible for a farmer to make a good living on as little as eighty acres if he also had a garden and some livestock; my, how things have changed! Farms of over 1000 acres are common and, sadly, it seems as though the family farm is rapidly becoming a thing of the past. I believe it will be a loss to our society when the small farmer, with his strong family values, totally gives way to the corporate managers.

The fertile Illinois prairie is part of the famed "Breadbasket of America" where much of our nation's food supply is grown.

My roots truly run deep in that rich, prairie soil!

Redmon, Illinois

If you travel west of Paris on Illinois State Route 133 for about ten miles, you come to the small town of Redmon, Illinois with a population of 199, according to the 2000 census. It seems to me like it has always been about that size. The main street is Oak Street, and the primary business in town is a large elevator operated by the Englum Grain Company. It is located on the south side of Oak Street and backs up to a railroad siding. There has been a grain elevator at that location as far back as I can remember. When I was a kid spending time in Redmon during harvest season, there would be long lines of trucks and wagons waiting to unload their cargos of golden grain. I can even remember a few wagons being pulled by horses. That makes me feel really old!

Immediately across the street, still stands my mother's girlhood home. It is a stately old frame, two-story house with a big front porch with pillars and an iron fence in front. It looks pretty much like it did when Mom lived there

Mom told us that when she was a little girl, she would crawl through an upstairs window and play with her dolls on the porch roof. One day she had her old dog Joe with her, and would toss him a ball that he would catch in his teeth. After a while the ball went over the edge of the porch and Joe jumped after it. He soon realized his mistake and let out a yelp. When he hit the ground, he just lay there and Mom started to cry. However, he soon began to stir around and only had the wind knocked out of him without sustaining any injuries.

Mom lived there with her brother, Ken, who was about four years older than Mom. Their parents were John Mason, Jr. and Bertha, who Jody and I called "Me and Meme Mason." Folks around Redmon called our grandfather "Johnny." They all lived with his parents, John Mason, Sr. and his wife, Caroline; she died in 1914 when Mom was only two. So, Mom never knew her grandmother on her dad's side. You'll remember that Johnny and Bertha met through a lonely-hearts ad in a magazine.

When Me Mason was a young man he operated a combination drug store and post office. The last time I was in Redmon, that building was still standing just southwest of the house, close to the street. The way old timers described the drug store, it was kind of like the modern day convenience store. When he was still single, he would look at the magazines coming through the post office and that is how he noticed Bertha's ad.

Once when he was young and single, some organization was selling raffle tickets for a white horse. Of course, Johnny, being a respected businessman in town, felt it necessary to participate in the raffle being conducted for a good cause, even though his father had strict rules against any kind of gambling. After the drawing was held, someone ran in the store and announced that he had won. Johnny was in sort of a panic and a customer in his store asked, "Hey, how much do you want for that horse?" Johnny replied, "TEN DOLLARS!" It turns out that the horse was worth about fifty dollars, but he was happy to be rid of it. The moral of that story: It pays to be in the right place at the right time.

My grandfather loved practical jokes. He would cut slices from a bar of yellow laundry soap and place the slices on the store counter with a sign that said, "Free Cheese." There would be a lot of spitting and bubbles floating around when his customers fell for the trick. They would usually run outside to the town pump and rinse out their mouths. I wonder if some never came back. But I guess they had to get used to his jokes since his store was the only game in town. In a later chapter, more of his tricks will be told.

Just east of the house, still stands an old brick bank building. I will tell a tale about it later on. Out in front of the house, along the sidewalk, was the town well where the residents of Redmon got their water for drinking and other uses. People used to pull their horses up to the adjacent tank to water them. I believe that the pump may still be there. There used to be a little tower nearby with a bell at the top, which could be sounded in case of fire.

Grandmother Bertha (Meme Mason) never liked living in Redmon, so in 1920, they finally moved to the house on West Crawford Street in Paris where I was born. My great grandfather, John Mason, Sr., was still living when they moved. He died in 1925.

A Prairie Cemetery

If you leave Redmon heading west on Rt. 133, in just over a mile you will come to a crossroad labeled Embarrass Cemetery Road or 400E. If you turn north on this road, in about a mile or so you will come to Embarrass Cemetery, which is on the west side of the road. I call this cemetery my ancestral burial ground.

My parents, Cecil and Edna Hall; her parents, John Jr. and Bertha Mason ("Me & Meme"); his parents, John Sr. and Caroline Mason; and her parents, John and Christina Gritz are all buried there, along with other relatives on Mom's dad's side. Next to my great grandparents' (John Sr., & Caroline) large granite gravestone, stands a small, slender red granite stone that marks the grave where their infant son is buried. He would have been my great uncle. John and

Caroline always said that a light in their lives went out when he died. My Grandfather's sister, Annie Stanley (my great aunt), is also buried there, I believe with her husband.

Christina Gritz came to America from Germany with her parents when she was about 8 years old, aboard a sailing ship. She told stories about how perilous the sea trip was. Then they had to get on a wagon train to travel to the Midwest. That was quite an undertaking and they must have been really motivated to come to the new world where freedom reined.

Twila and I plan to be buried in this cemetery near my parents. Sister Jody and her husband Joe Kurchak also have plots there, as do my brother Gary and his wife Judy.

There is a frame church located in the northeast corner of the cemetery near the road. The last I knew, Sunday services were still being held there. This church was once a classic country church with a steeple and bell but it has long been remodeled. I liked it better before the remodeling. When our parents were visiting the cemetery, Jody and I would play around the church. The door was never locked. We played the piano and pretended like we were preaching sermons. We were always careful to not leave any messes or bother anything.

We always noticed a rope coming down from the ceiling in the vestibule with the end coiled up and hanging on a hook on the wall. We knew it was how they rang the bell but never touched it, until one-day curiosity got the best of us, and we dared each other to pull the rope. I wanted to show my big sister how brave I was so I gave the rope a good healthy tug. Well, the bell tolled, going *DING-DONG* and it scared us half to death! I didn't know it would be so loud! We thought sure someone would come to check on the church so we went running as far as we could from it. Nobody came to check so I was glad that the bell hadn't tolled for me.

Mom told the story in which, years ago, there was a funeral being held in the church when a very loud bang was heard like someone hitting the side of the church with a flat board. Some men ran outside to see what caused the noise but found nothing. The funeral was resumed and, after a while, the same noise was heard again, only louder. Mom said that the diseased had promised to try to communicate after his death so it kind of makes you wonder. They never found out what caused it and it was never heard again. I'm sure there was a reasonable explanation for the cause of the noise. I hope so!

Nowadays, there is a community park north of the church property. It used to be a woodlot but the underbrush has been cleared away to make room for playground equipment and picnic tables. Since I like kids so much, I think it will be kind of nice to be buried where the sound of children playing in the park can be heard.

Mom and Dad always planted flowers on the relatives' graves each year before Memorial Day. It was my job to walk down to the old iron bridge across Catfish Creek and draw water with a rope and bucket. Sometimes, they were ready to water the flowers and there would be no Danny. I would be leaning on the bridge railing, watching the turtles and throwing rocks in the water. My teachers usually told my parents that I was a dreamer, but that I always got my work done. I would come running when they called and usually managed to spill a lot of water so I would have to go back for a refill.

Mom once told our pastor, Rev. W. at the first Baptist Church in Paris that her little Danny was a dreamer. He patted my head and said, "Son, you keep right on dreaming. This world needs more dreamers." That trait served me well in later years when I was involved in exploration geology. I seemed to be able to vividly imagine the underground structures that might be present in a given area after I became familiar with the geology of the region.

Marion's Farm

During his lifetime, my great grandfather, John Mason Sr. accumulated some farmland in the Redmon / Brocton area. When Mom lived with her grandparents in Redmon, money was scarce because so much was being invested in property, and she could always tell when another farm was being purchased because there would be no sugar on the table. Upon John Sr.'s death in 1925, my grandfather, John Jr. ("Me Mason") and his sister, Aunt Annie, inherited the farms and my grandfather ended up with three of them. During the great depression he lost one of the farms, an event that bothered him for the rest of his life.

The farm that I remember contained 120 acres, located a couple of miles or so northwest of Embarrass Cemetery. Marion Jones farmed it for my grandfather and my parents after they inherited it in 1943. My mother's brother, Ken, inherited the other farm. We always referred to the 120 acres as "Marion's Farm."

It had a typical farmstead with a red barn, a double corncrib with a driveway through the middle, and another shed. There was an old freight car behind the house that was used for a garage and junk storage. Marion kept his tractor and other equipment in a lean-to addition at the rear. There was an outhouse northeast of the house with a big garden between it and the house. I seem to remember that there was a chicken house just north of the garden.

The farm well was located about 200 feet west of the house, about five feet from the barnyard fence, a terrible place for a well. There was a hand pump for the well with a tin cup hanging on the pump. The livestock tank was located in the barnyard, just across the fence. Everyone who came around drank out of that cup. The water tasted very strong from minerals, and new victims would make a face when they took their first drink. Marion liked the taste of the water and joked that the minerals were good for your system and would keep your intestines functioning well. He might have been on to something because I never saw any constipated pigs or cows around there.

When I was a kid, I wondered if the taste could be from being so close to the barnyard, but the water was always cold and refreshing on a hot summer day. Dad must have had the same concerns because he had the water tested for bacteria periodically. It always tested pure.

Marion and his wife, Dorothy, lived in the house on the farm with their daughter, Pat. Marion was one of the best farmers around that part of the country. You never saw a single weed sticking up from his soybean fields and I have seen him stop his car and run over into the field to pull a weed. After the corn got too tall to cultivate, we would sometimes go over and help him walk the field with a hoe. That was always great fun, to be in a cornfield on a hot summer day. The edges of the leaves were sharp enough to cut your skin if they hit you just right. Marion was the only farmer I knew of who went to this extreme.

When I was just a little shaver, Marion would let me sit in his lap and steer his John Deere tractor. I loved doing that and would tell everyone that I could drive a tractor. Later on, he gave me the nickname "Abner" because I had big feet that reminded him of the comic strip character Lil Abner. His wife Dorothy died giving birth to a son, who also perished. Marion took their deaths very hard and was in deep grief for a long time. He eventually married a lady named Opal.

He was so honest that at harvest time, he would always throw an extra load of corn in the half of the crib that belonged to my parents. Dad caught him doing that and chewed him out.

Marion's daughter Pat was a tomboy deluxe, and we were buddies. We had all the fun that kids could have on a farm. One of the activities we enjoyed was climbing up inside the corncrib and dropping feet first into a wagonload of grain. We would go in up to our waists and the grain would fly everywhere. Dad saw us doing this once and told

Marion that we were wasting grain. Marion replied, "Yes, but kids have to have fun." I thought Marion was an all-right guy!

Dad loved guns and always brought his .22 pistol when he went to the farm. There were often other farmers that came around while he was there. They would get to talking and Dad would challenge them to throw their cap up in the air to see if he could hit it with his pistol. They usually fell for the bait because they didn't believe anyone could hit an object in the air with a pistol. One fellow threw his hat so high that the wind caught it and sent it sailing. I thought sure Dad would miss it but it came down with a hole through the bill. I never saw him miss, so there were a lot of farmers in that part of the country walking around with bullet holes in their hats.

It was so exciting to go to the farm during harvest time. I loved to ride on the combine and I would stand by the hopper and watch the golden grain pour in. There were usually insect parts and other extraneous material coming in with the grain. I noticed that sometimes a grasshopper's upper rear leg would be almost identical to the size of an oat grain. I wondered how they could be separated during the processing into cereal and I convinced myself that it was impossible.

When Mom served oatmeal, I always examined it to determine if it contained any insect parts. I would take the tip of my spoon and fish out any dark substances and give them a close scrutiny. Mom didn't appreciate me doing that, and let me know that she didn't. I was never able to come up with a positive insect identification, although sometimes the objects looked mighty suspicious.

When Mom died in 1994, Jody and I inherited Marion's farm, minus 5 acres that included the farmstead, which my parents had sold to Marion and Opal some years earlier. My brother Gary and his wife Judy inherited other property to make up their share. After about a year, Twila and I sold our share. It was a very difficult decision because that farm had been in our family for over 100 years. However, ours was the last generation that could allow it to be kept together, and it would have become very fragmented upon our deaths. The timing was right to let it go and we don't regret selling it. Jody and Joe kept a 20-acre plot for a while before eventually selling it.

I still have fond memories of that prairie farm.

Chapter 6

Withdrawals From the Memory Bank

Loving parents, what a treasure!
A thought of them brings such pleasure.

Misty memories from bygone years.
We think of them, eyes filled with tears.

Lessons taught on what is right.
We try to remember them in the night.

The Author

This chapter contains an assortment of memories from my childhood. They are mostly pleasant memories but I become nostalgic when I think about some of my loved ones who have passed. So my eyeballs may sweat a little while I pass along some of these tidbits.

Memories are special gifts and they become even more precious when you share them. So, come with me if you will, and let's continue our stroll down memory lane.

Winter Fun

While many adults dreaded the harsh Illinois winters, practically every kid looked forward to them. The freezing rain and snow sometimes made my life miserable when I had my paper route but I still enjoyed the winters.

Almost all boys, and some girls, had to have a sled with runners. We soon found out that the short sleds were much easier to tote around and were actually faster than the long ones. If you kept the runners waxed, those things would go like the wind. Although I wanted a short one, I had to make do with one of medium length that the folks had bought for Jody before I was born.

The streets were often icy and you could take a run and jump on your sled and go a long distance. Our town wasn't very hilly so we had to do the best we could. There was an overhead bridge across a railroad track near Mayo School and the older kids would go there for a long sled coast, but you had to be careful of cars coming over the bridge.

It was rumored that there was a hill somewhere out by the country club that was good for coasting but I never checked it out. It supposedly had a railroad track at the bottom and it was said that some daredevil kids would play chicken with the trains and see how close they could cross in front of a moving train. There was a story going around that a kid actually slid across the track under a moving freight car. If all the stories were true, it is a miracle that no one was killed out there.

I did indulge in an activity that was dangerous but a lot of fun. When the streets were really icy, the cars had to go fairly slow. We would wait at the edge of a street and, when a car came by, we ran after it and jumped on our sleds and grabbed hold of the back bumper. If the conditions were just right, you could go for blocks like this. Sometimes you would see three or four kids at the back of a car. You tried to get on the side opposite the tailpipe for obvious reasons, but you had to take what was available. Many drivers would stop and chase you away from their cars but others didn't mind letting kids have fun this way. One of the dangers was that you could slide underneath the car and a back wheel might run over you. I never came close to having that happen.

Then there were the snow forts and snowball fights. It was common for a bunch of kids to form teams. You tried to stockpile a stack of snowballs behind your fort in preparation for battle. It was not wise to go out on the battlefield between the forts to gather more ammunition during an actual battle. We got pretty serious with those battles, and the air would be filled with snowballs. Of course, during the war, we imagined we were soldiers fighting an actual battle.

For the younger kids, there was the fun of making snowmen. Sometimes the older kids would build anatomically correct ones and you could easily distinguish the males from the females. Usually an adult would come along and alter them to the unisex variety. Kids can be very creative so I won't mention some of the snow characters they came up with. I don't want this story to be x- rated!

Later on, in a cold winter, when Twin Lakes were frozen over, ice-skating was a favorite activity. On a busy Saturday afternoon, the skaters, with their scarves of various colors flying behind them, would provide a postcard-like scene.

One guy came up with a sail and he could actually go faster on the ice than the velocity of the wind when he sailed crosswind. He was fun to watch. Once snow covered the ice, it would end his wind skating.

An Illinois winter provided good times for most folks of all ages.

Into the Woods

When I was a boy, there were two seasons I looked forward to with great anticipation: the mushroom season in the spring, and the squirrel season in the fall. I really enjoyed spending time in the woods and did so at every opportunity.

From about mid-April until Mother's Day, the tasty morel mushrooms could be found. It was common to drive past a prime wood-lot around Paris and see several cars parked along the country road. Once in awhile, you could see someone emerge from the woods with a paper bag filled with the prized morsels. If you stopped them and inquired as to exactly where they found them, you would never get a straight answer. Everyone had his own coveted, secret mushroom patch. However, the morels were extremely elusive, never growing where you expected them to be.

Morels blended in well with the forest vegetation and everyone seemed to have a favorite hunting technique. Some folks carried a walking stick to scrape leaves away from an area and to bend the branching plants over to look under them. I noticed that they commonly grew around Jack-in-the-pulpit plants, so if I came across a patch of them, I would check it out thoroughly. I can't tell you any more without revealing too much about my secret techniques. Anyway, sharp eyes were a must, which is why kids often won the family's picking contests.

One of our favorite mushroom spots was east of Paris. I think it was called Eads Woods. We always had pretty good luck there. The morels must grow awfully fast, because one time Mom stepped out of the car and left a footprint in the soft earth and, when we returned a couple of hours later, there was a mushroom growing right in the middle of it.

There were lots of hickory trees in that woods, and Jody and I loved to find a young sapling and shinny up near the top. The wood was so springy that, if you picked the proper size, it would bend over without breaking until your feet touched the ground. Then you gave a little shove with your feet and the tree would go back up and bend over the opposite way. It was kind of like a tee-ter-totter but more fun. I guess the springy nature of the hickory wood was why Native Americans used them to make bows.

When you were out in the woods, you needed to be careful of snakes. We pretty well knew which ones were poisonous, but they were rare. Dad once caught a blacksnake about as long as he was tall. While he held it with a grip behind its head, it threw a coil around his wrist, then another one, then another one, and began to apply constricting pressure. Dad used his left hand to unwind the coils, which was kind of difficult to do. He quickly let the snake go because it had stopped the blood circulation in his right hand. I never saw him fool around with another blacksnake. I imagine that ole snake had quite a tale to tell to his buddies.

When we took our morels home, we split them down the middle and soaked them for a while in salt water to remove all the bugs. Then we rolled each half in egg batter and fried them in butter. I am salivating just thinking about the taste of them.

Last spring, our daughter Laura sent us a big box of morels from Montana and we fried about a fourth of them and dried the rest. We discovered that, when you soak the dried ones in water over-night, they return almost to their original size and taste the same.

Squirrel hunting season came in about the middle of September in Illinois, as I recall. Even when I was just a little guy, Dad would take me squirrel hunting with him. How I treasured those hunts. There were many hickory, walnut and oak trees in the wood lots around Paris and the hunting for fox squirrels was excellent.

We would walk quietly through the woods but, if we saw a squirrel and he saw or heard us, he would move around to the opposite side of the tree where Dad couldn't get a shot. Dad would have me stand in one spot while he made his way around to the other side of the tree and the squirrel would come around to my side of the tree. When he was ready, he would wave to me and I would give a nearby bush a shake and the squirrel would move around to his side. His little Remington, .22 short, semi-automatic rifle would crack and I would hear the distinctive *thump* when the dead squirrel hit the ground, more often than not, shot in the head. Dad always tried to save meat by making headshots.

The meals he provided for his family were welcome additions to our menu because it meant that Mom would have to spend less on groceries, and any savings she could realize was welcome news in those days, so soon after the great depression. I loved fried squirrel, mashed potatoes with gravy and I would greatly enjoy a meal like that right now.

I longed for the day when I would be old enough to hunt with the little Remington. That time came when I was about eleven years old, and I was ecstatic. I vividly remember the first squirrel I bagged, shot in the head! I really felt like an accomplished hunter.

When I started hunting with the rifle, Dad took to hunting with his .22 pistol. Believe it or not, he made head shots with it also. I had to be careful not to tell that around too much because my friends would think I was lying.

One of the wood lots where we hunted was owned by an elderly gentleman who loved fried squirrel but was too feeble to hunt. Often, when we finished our hunt on his land, we would give him a couple of squirrels and stay long enough to skin and clean them for him. I'll never forget the time when Dad laid out five squirrels and the old man's mouth dropped open when he saw they were all shot in the head. Dad didn't have the heart to tell him that they were all shot with a pistol.

Those were great times and even today, when I hear a blue jay call, or a crow caw, or a squirrel bark on a warm autumn day, my thoughts wander back to those happy times in the woods with Dad. How I would love to go hunting with him just one more time, maybe someday in the by and by.

"Under the wide and starry sky
Dig the grave and let me lie.
Glad did I live and gladly die,
And laid me down with a will.

This be the verse you gave for me:
Here he lies where he longs to be.
Home is the sailor, home from the sea,
And the hunter home from the hill."
Epitaph: Robert Lewis Stevenson, 1850-1894

Into the Fields

The upland game bird season opened in November, as I remember, and this was another anticipated date. Dad would take the whole family to the red clover fields and hedgerows out on the prairie northwest of Paris to hunt pheasants. There were many pheasants in those days but these days, their population is significantly diminished.

He would have us fan out across the field so as to flush out the birds roosting there. Sometimes, Jody would go back and forth in front of us to help flush the birds. They made a loud noise when they took off that startled you if you weren't expecting it. The roosters would usually cackle when they flushed. I guess they were scolding us for disturbing their comfort. The Chinese ring neck roosters are beautiful birds and only the roosters were legal game. The hens don't have the brilliant colors and long tails that the roosters have, and were protected.

After I got my BB gun, I took it hunting and would shoot at the flushing pheasants. Strangely enough, nobody laughed at me for doing that. Dad hunted with a 16 gage, Model 12 Winchester and Mom carried a single shot 20 gage. The birds would startle her so much that I don't think she ever shot it.

Later on, Dad bought a bird dog, which made hunting and finding dead game a lot more efficient. Her name was Lizzie and she was an outstanding pointer. She would scout the area in front of the hunters with her nose to the ground. When she got near a roosting bird, she would freeze on point and you had to go in front of her and flush the bird. On cold, frosty mornings, you had to practically kick the birds out with your toe. Lizzie had such a wonderful nose that she almost always found dead birds and would retrieve them. It was truly a joy to watch Lizzie work.

Pheasants were also an important mainstay in the diet of our family during hunting season. They tasted a little bit like chicken (doesn't everything?), but were all dark meat.

Dad also quail hunted in the brush country, usually with his friends. The walking was so strenuous that he didn't take the whole family. He could usually only go on short quail hunting trips because of his bad knees. Sometimes he tried to hunt with his friends all day but he would be miserable and would commonly be laid up for a while.

On an ideal quail hunt, a covey of birds would flush; and, if you were good with a shotgun, you could bag two or three birds out of the covey. Then, if you watched which way they flew, you could go there and work the singles. I think quail hunting was Lizzie's favorite sport.

Fun with Nitro

On Marion's farm, there were a few stumps left from an old hedge-row and they were an unneeded obstacle for his plowing and cultivating. They were particularly troublesome when he tried to consolidate two fields and the stumps were still there, separating the plots. Not only that, but there was a huge granite boulder out in the middle of a field that was dropped there when the last glacier melted.

One day, Dad brought home a case of dynamite with all the accessories such as caps and fuses. Dynamite was much easier to obtain in those days and you could just go to a lumberyard to purchase as much as you needed. They would usually ask what you were going to use it for, and you simply had to tell them. I guess if you told them you were going to blow up a school, they might not sell it to you. Life was so much simpler then!

I considered myself a very lucky boy to be included on that stump removal expedition, but Mom was very worried. Dad tried to reassure her by telling her it would be OK and that he would take good care of me. I was so excited about going that Mom didn't want to disappoint me by throwing a fuss about it. I could hardly wait until the following Saturday, *D-Day* I called it, which meant dynamite day to me.

The appointed day came, and we headed over to Marion's farm. I could hardly wait to get there. I had seen explosions in movies but had never seen one live and up close.

On the way over, I was a little nervous about riding in the car with dynamite in the trunk but Dad finally convinced me it was safe. Marion was waiting when we arrived and was pleased to report that he had tunneled under each of the stumps in preparation for the placement of the charges.

I am pretty sure that neither Marion nor my dad had much previous experience with demolition, so I thought to myself that this operation might be interesting to watch. But they sure acted like they knew what they were doing.

Dad took a stick of 40% dynamite and punched a hole in the side of it with a pencil. This made me nervous again. He then took a cap, stuck one end of the fuse in it, crimped it with his teeth, and inserted the cap into the stick of dynamite. I thought he was very brave to do this. He then placed it, along with a couple of other sticks, under the first stump with about three feet of fuse attached. He lit the fuse and we all ran a good distance away and waited with great anticipation.

It seemed like an eternity, but it finally blew with a great cloud of dust and Dad vowed to use a shorter fuse for the next stump. We walked up to the stump to view the results. It had blown a lot of dirt away from the roots of the stump and left only a few strands of roots remaining. Marion said he could easily cut it loose, haul it off, and fill the hole. He had a way of making every job sound easy.

The remainder of the stumps went about the same way and the guys were really feeling like demolition experts. There must have been about six or so stumps. The big boulder was next in line to feel the wrath of the demolition team. Dad was pleased to discover that Marion had tunneled under it also. He was a worker's worker!

They placed a huge charge under the rock with a good long fuse to give them time to get a long way off because they thought they would have to dodge flying rock fragments. To make a long story short, the fuse was lit and we all waited a couple of hundred yards upwind.

The explosion came with a huge cloud of dust but no rock pieces could be seen leaving the premises. When the smoke and dust had cleared away, no trace of the rock could be seen. It had just disappeared! Marion and Dad just looked at each other for what seemed a minute or so. When we walked up to the scene, there was a huge crater with the boulder sitting on the bottom. The blast had revealed a crescent shaped inclusion on the side of the rock that seemed to make it look like it was smiling at us. I had to laugh.

The rock was so big that only the tip of it was sticking out of the hole, enough to still snag a plow. There seemed to be two options from which to choose: either we could dig under it again and place another charge, hoping to blast it deeper, or the upper portion could be dealt with. They chose to let it be until they could ponder the situation for a while.

Dad must have talked to an expert before we came back the next Saturday to give the smiling rock another treatment. He placed another huge charge on top of the rock then covered it with a damp mudpack. When the charge went off, we saw small rock fragments flying away. A close inspection revealed that about the top third of the rock had been fragmented into pieces small enough to be scraped to the side of the boulder, thus providing ample clearance for a plow.

Marion was faced with a sizable job of filling in the crater, but he seemed to be happy. I was happy too because I had learned how to, and how not to blow stumps and boulders. You never know when a little scrap of knowledge might come in handy.

Comic Books and the Tree House

When I had my paper route, I was really into comic books and had a little bit of disposable income to spend on them. My very favorite hero was *Captain Marvel*, but I also liked *Superman* and *Plastic Man*. *Dick Tracy* was also right there at the top. I thought his wrist radio was something too difficult to ever manufacture. Comic books had a way of predicting the future;

just witness *Buck Rogers*, another favorite.

I would tie a dish drying cloth around my neck like a cape and pretend I was Captain Marvel. The only attempts I made at flying were when I jumped from the roofs of chicken houses, yelling, "Shazam!" The flights were fine but the landings were a little rough. I only did this a few times but it might have been enough to make my feet as flat as pancakes. In later years, I was almost refused entry into the Navy, but I convinced them that my flat feet didn't bother me.

I wish I still had those old comic books. Some of them would be worth a fortune now.

One of my favorite things was to climb up to my tree house and lie there among the greenery reading comic books. I called it a tree house but it was just a wooden platform about thirty or so feet up in a maple tree that stood beside the alley. To get up there I had to shinny up a rope. I could climb a rope almost as fast as I could climb a ladder. The rope had one major advantage over a ladder because when you got up there, you could pull the rope up after you and keep unwanted guests away. I had a bucket tied to the bottom of the rope in which to place objects to be pulled up to the tree house.

Once in awhile, one or two of Mrs. Fisk's felines would come visit me in my lofty domain. They probably wanted to check me out to see if I was planning some treachery against them. I hate to disappoint you but I treated them as guests. Honestly! I distinctly remember letting one of her cats eat part of a peanut butter and jelly sandwich. She probably went to do her business in my sandbox after she ate it.

I had a good friend named Ron who lived a short bike ride away. He spent a lot of time with me just playing basketball and hanging around. He could go up a rope about as fast as I could, so we spent considerable time in the maple tree reading comic books. We traded them back and forth so that we always had a fresh supply of reading material.

One day we were poking around in a box of junk at Me Mason's place and found an old pulley. The spool had seized up from rust and corrosion, but when we gave it a good dose of oil, it turned freely. We knew that there must be a way for a couple of boys to have fun with that old pulley.

We got our heads together and came up with an idea for an elevator to transport us up to the tree house. We already had a long enough length of sturdy rope that fit the pulley. So we went to work building a working elevator. There was a big limb positioned a little more than head high above the tree house, so we tied the pulley to that limb, which would enable the ropes coming out of the pulley to hang about two feet from the edge of the platform.

A seat, like a swing seat, was fashioned on one end of the rope and a large wooden box was tied to the other end, like you would tie a cargo container. Ron and I were of about the same weight, so we figured that all we had to do was to put rocks and bricks in the box to balance one boy's weight almost exactly. We reasoned that it would then be easy to sit in the seat and use our hands on the other rope to help our nearly weightless body go up and down.

Ron wanted to go first and so did I, so we flipped a coin to decide who had the privilege of taking the first trip. We imagined ourselves sort of like test pilots. The heavy box was on the ground and the seat hung just off the edge of the tree house.

Ron got up in the tree and climbed into the seat. Nothing happened! He took hold of the rope attached to the box and began feeding himself along, going hand over hand. We planned that, when he came down, I would exchange places with him and ride back up. The elevator seemed to work exactly as designed and we felt like a couple of geniuses; you can probably guess what happened next, something like what could happen in a

Three Stooges movie.

Well, the box started swinging and swung against the trunk of the tree. The box disassembled which dumped the rocks and bricks, which made the elevator come down very fast. Ron hit the ground with a *thump* and didn't move. I wanted to get away! But I ran over to check on him, thinking that he must be dead. He finally opened one eye and began to stir around. It had just knocked the wind out of him and he was not injured. I breathed a sigh of relief.

Thus ended our career in elevator design, and we went back to climbing the rope.

Wallpaper Magic

Our parents must have loved wallpaper because all of the rooms, with the exception of one, in our house in Northwest Paris were wallpapered. The lone exception was a small-enclosed back porch.

For wallpaper jobs, such as cleaning and repapering, they always called on Gene P., a professional paperhanger. He told us kids to just call him Gene. We had a coal-fired furnace that heated the house pretty well but it was dirty heat. They had to get Gene to clean the walls fairly often. He used a kind of putty product that he would knead from time to time so as to keep a fresh surface exposed for the cleaning. I usually didn't notice the paper being very dirty until he took the first swipe with a hunk of the cleaner. The difference it made was awesome. He used to give Jody and me little wads of cleaner and let us draw stuff on the wall before he got to that area. He was good with kids.

Gene was so good at putting up wallpaper that he was fun for a kid to watch. There was no wasted motion, and he could do a room in no time at all. He made the job look so deceptively easy that it led my folks astray. Being astray for a wallpapering job is no place to be.

It must have rankled them to see one room un-papered because they talked often about having Gene do the little back room. But they finally decided they could do it themselves if they did it exactly like he did. This was a fatal flaw in their thinking process!

They got their nerve up and prepared to tackle the job one Independence Day when Dad was off work. They somehow came up with all the tools and material they needed to do the job. Maybe Gene loaned them the stuff to teach them a lesson. They learned a good lesson for sure.

The room had maybe 150 square feet or so and had low ceilings. I thought it would be a quick job so that they could take us kids somewhere fun in the afternoon. Wrong! I was judging the operation by Gene's standards.

Every Fourth of July in those days, Paris had a hot-air balloon ascension where the guy would ride it up to a fairly high altitude on a trapeze-like bar, then parachute to earth. Then in the evening, there was always a fireworks display out at Twin Lakes Park. Sometimes the whole family would get in Dad's boat and he would row us out to the middle of the lake to watch the display. There was also a parade in the afternoon and, when I got to be a boy scout later on, I could march in it. I looked forward to taking in all the festivities that day.

They stripped the room, put a sheet of plywood on sawhorses, cut some paper the proper lengths, placed them face down on the plywood, and mixed the paste. This was just the way Gene did it and they really acted like they knew what they were doing.

Dad brushed the paste onto the first strip of paper, turned to the wall, put the upper edge in place next to the ceiling, used the big stiff brush to force all the air pockets out, and pressed it against the wall. This was just the way Gene did it and I was impressed. I thought, wow, this job will be over in record time and we can go have some family fun.

Dad turned around to paste up the next strip when something caught my eye. The top of the first strip slowly detached and began rolling down the wall at an accelerating speed. It ended up looking ever so innocent on the floor. Dad finished pasting strip number two and turned to position it against the first strip. No first strip!

He stopped motionless for a few seconds to ascertain what had happened to strip numeral uno. He said something but I can't remember what it was. He quickly put both strips back on the wall and brushed them in. When he was preparing the third strip, the first two strips slowly made their way to the floor.

Dad had been pretty patient until this point but his calmness gave way to anger. I was asked to leave the house, and the last I saw of Dad; he had a strip of pasted wallpaper around his neck. His face was all red like it was going to explode and Mom was standing there wringing her hands. I had never seen him quite this angry.

I went out to the back of the property, thinking my world, as I knew it, might come to an end. I was pretty upset. I remember looking out in the distance and seeing the hot-air balloon go up. I stood there and watched until I saw the parachute come down and knew the guy was OK.

I fooled around for a while then climbed the rope to my tree house and tried to make some sense out of a comic book. After what seemed like a very long time, Mom came out of the back door looking happy. She announced that the job was finally done and we could still make it to the fireworks show.

I went in to inspect the job and tried not to laugh. The edges of the paper curled just a little and did not fit up very well. Dad usually did a workmanlike job at anything he attempted but this was a glaring exception.

When Mom told about it later, she said that as soon as Dad put each strip up, she had to stand there with a board and hold the top against the wall until the paste set up enough to do the job. I'm surprised they finished the job as quickly as they did. I never saw them try to put up wallpaper again.

In retrospect, after doing some wallpapering myself, I realize that they should have sized the walls before trying to get the paste to stick. I wonder if Gene "forgot" to tell them about sizing.

Later on, we got a lot of laughs out of the wallpaper job but it was sure not very funny at the time. Even Dad could see the humor in it eventually.

Christmas Culinary

Dad's parents, Tom and Virginia Hall, lived on North Street in Paris, about three blocks from Vance School. Jody and I called her "Meme Hall" and we just called him Tom.

Sometimes I walked over to their house after school if the weather was too miserable to walk all the way home, or if I just wanted a diversion. I visited with her while I played with Uncle Jack's old toys. He had several cast iron trucks and cars that would now be antiques or at least collector's items. It is that way with many of the toys I used to play with.

They lived in a story and a half, bungalow style house with a big front porch. There was a porch swing there and I would swing on it while watching the happenings on North Street.

The only heat came from a coal stove on one end of the big dining room. I often played around the stove on cold winter days. The only heat for the upstairs bedroom came through a hole in the bedroom floor covered with a grate. The bedroom was very cold in the winter and very hot in the summer. The grated hole in the floor fascinated Jody and me, and we found it great fun to huddle around it up in the bedroom and eavesdrop on adult conversations taking place in the living room below. Sometimes I would fit paper airplanes through the grate and well-designed ones could sometimes sail around the lower room for a while.

Tom was a hardworking carpenter, and when he was home, he was usually sacked out on a daybed near the heating stove. He worked as a meat cutter a number of years before he became a carpenter, and I thought him a man of many talents. He could build nice things out of little more than scraps, and once made Jody a nice doll chest.

Tom drove an old Model A Ford coupe, which his wife hated with a passion. He kept his tools and supplies in the trunk so that there was never room for anything else. There was usually a long brass tube strapped to the side, and I wondered what he did with the thing. I later found out that he used it to collect samples of grain from railroad cars at the cereal mill to be tested for quality. He would stick the tube down through the grain and twist the inner sleeve, which opened the ports to collect samples from the entire depth of the load.

Every Christmas, Meme Hall had the whole family in for a noontime feast of turkey with all the trimmings, and I do mean trimmings! I have never seen such a table full of food before or since. I always had to leave my new Christmas toys to go to these meals. This was a real sacrifice for me, and I would fuss about it all the way to their house. My folks finally decreed that I could bring one or two small toys with me. However, that carried the risk of my cousins tearing them up before I had a chance to do it myself. I once took a cast iron alligator because I thought it was one toy that couldn't be damaged. That observation was true, but one of my younger cousins grabbed it

90

and began hitting people with it. Mom had to confiscate it until we left.

Dad's older sister, Opal, was married and divorced three or four times and ended up remarried to her first husband, Paul. One Christmas, she had just married an older man. They were supposed to be coming for the big meal but were running late, so the meal was delayed to wait for them; the adults were sitting in the living room talking about adult things.

Jody and I became bored with all this conversation and took our leave. We thought it might be a good time to do a little eavesdropping so we quietly made our way upstairs to the bedroom with the hole in the floor. Not long after we got settled by the grating, the conversation turned to Aunt Opal and her new husband. We soon became bored and almost went away, but the conversation was becoming more interesting.

We listened there for a while then heard our grandmother say, "I hear that Opal's new husband gave her an old, used organ for a wedding present." Her remark unleashed a storm of laughter but it flew right over our heads. We just looked at each other and shrugged our shoulders. Years later, I understood what she meant by that remark. Opal and her husband finally arrived and we enjoyed the usual great meal.

Pigs and Poultry

When I was nine years old, Dad came home one day with some news for me. He said that he had been out to visit his friend, Fred Powers, on his farm and that he had a sow with a nice new litter of pigs, except one of them was a runt and was getting nudged out of the way by the other pigs when he tried to suckle. He said that the runt would soon die unless someone fed it separately.

My grandfather, Me Mason, had given up raising chickens a couple of years or so earlier, and his chicken lot and houses were just sitting there vacant. Dad told me that if I could deal Fred out of that pig, I could take it under my wing and raise it in the chicken lot. I thought about it for a while and then accepted the offer.

I met with Mr. Powers one-on-one a few days later, looked at the pig, and asked him if I could buy it. He quoted me a price and I told him it was too high for such a sorry little critter. We dickered back and forth for a while and I ended up with it. He later told Dad that he really got a kick out of dealing with me and that I drove a hard bargain.

I made a comfortable place for the little fellow in one of the chicken houses and kept him locked in so that a predatory animal couldn't have him for breakfast. I named him Oscar and bottle-fed him twice a day. It kept me busy feeding and cleaning up after him. The bottle-feeding method took lots of time, so I introduced him to solid food as soon as I could. Every morning and evening, I mixed some of his ground feed with water and poured it in his little trough. When he got big enough, I opened the door and let him have the run of the lot. He seemed happy and grew quickly.

In about six or seven months, Oscar grew to about 200 pounds and the day finally came for him to go to market. I put it off as long as I could. We had become buddies, and I tearfully told him goodbye.

I learned a lot from raising that pig and realized a pretty fair profit. The most important thing I learned was that you should never name an animal that will be eaten.

About this time, Jody decided she could once again populate the "chicken ranch" to earn some money. So, one day she and Mom came home from the hatchery with three or four boxes of baby chicks. There are few things as cute as a baby chick and there was a lot of "ooh-ing" and "ah-ing." That continuous cheeping kind of irritated me. After my experience with the old white rooster, I thought the only good chickens were fried or served with dumplings.

Jody and Mom made a nice home for the chicks and hooked up a brooder hood to keep them warm. I think they used a light bulb for heat. The chicks had a little feed trough and water dish and seemed to be happy. However, Jody found out that there is a high mortality rate with baby chicks. When she fed them each day, it was not uncommon to find one or two with their feet in the air.

She mourned each death, and once recruited me to help prepare a burial service. She handled all the details including a short message for all the chick's relatives. We then took the matchbox casket out and lowered it into the little grave. I tried my best to offer a decent rendition of "Taps" on my Boy Scout bugle. I must say that I did not exhibit the same degree of grief as my sister did.

She was very faithful in caring for her chickens, and most of them grew up to frying size. I loved to hear people describe them as "fryers," and hoped she could contribute a few for family meals. After all, we all had a part in raising those critters.

The day came when Jody declared that the fryers were ready to be sold, so she somehow advertised them and the customers came. Raise chickens and they will come! The buyers could go to the chicken yard with her and have their pick. I could never understand the criteria some of the customers used for selecting their next meal. I thought that if the bird was really active, the meat might have stringy muscles. On the other hand, if it looked lazy, it might indicate it wasn't feeling well. I could never predict which one the buyers would choose.

Some of them took a long time in making their selection, almost like they were choosing a child to adopt. When they chose more than one, Jody was happy. She then had to fetch the ones they chose. She would take the wire chicken catcher, with a hook on one end, and go chasing the selected chickens. She sold them by the pound, so she had to tie their legs together and weigh them. I thought that collecting the money would make her think it was all worth it, and I feared she would buy another batch of chicks and start all over.

The truth was that she was sick of the whole deal and thought there must be a better way to earn money. She never again got into chicken ranching.

Back to Pigs

My grandfather, Tom Hall, managed to raise a few hogs at the back of their big lot on North Street. These days, that could never be attempted inside the city limits. Things were just different back then. Everyone was just trying to make do and get by, and had the attitude to live and let live. Some of his neighbors did mention it from time to time but didn't seriously object. Maybe his gifts of sausages and bacon kept them appeased.

Every year, Tom and Meme Hall butchered a hog for their own use. Our family always went out and helped process the meat. Meme Hall cured the hams by placing them in a washtub and rubbing them with a mixture of brown sugar, salt, and spices. They were then hung in an unheated room at the back of the house. It could be that they smoked them in there.

It was Tom's job to grind the sausage. He jacked up one corner of his Model A Ford and positioned the sausage grinder with its axel aligned with the axel of the vehicle. He placed the handle of the crank between the wire spokes of the wheel. He then put the Ford in gear, pulled out the hand throttle a little bit and let out the clutch. The grinder began to turn which seemed miraculous to me. I thought he was the smartest grandpa in the whole, wide world!

While he was grinding sausage, Meme Hall was preparing the natural casings. She would never tell me where they came from for fear that I wouldn't eat the sausages. She stripped them of their contents and washed them thoroughly in a lye solution that was evil smelling. She then took a hose and rinsed them out, forcing the water through the inside.

They used a sausage stuffing apparatus and it was my job to work the lever. The strings of sausages were then hung with the hams. They sure made delicious eating no matter where the casings came from.

Sometimes, she would ask me if I would like a balloon to play with and I always said I did because I didn't know that they didn't just keep a supply of them for their grandkids. When I wasn't looking, she washed the hog bladder the same way she did the sausage casings, blew it up and tied the openings. I had fun with the "balloons" and was bouncing one down the street one day when a kid asked me were I got it. I replied, "I don't know, but you have to help butcher a hog to get one."

Figure 1. My mother, sister and me in 1935 with Pat the dog. I don't remember the cat's name.

Figure 2. Dad and me in 1935.

Figure 3. Jody and me in 1939.

Figure 4. Jody and me in 1942.

Figure 5. Me with our dog, Topper, next to the tree with my tree house. The big garden is in the background and my grandparents' house across the garden ("Me & Meme Mason").

Figure 6. When I was a patrol boy at Vance School in 6th grade. My job was to help younger kids across the busy streets. I thought I was really important. I guess maybe I was.

Figure 7. The siblings: Barbara ("Jody"), Dan, and Gary.
Taken in Branson, Missouri in 2006.

Figure 8. Mom & Dad in the early years.

Figure 9. Mom dressed for the play, "Henpecked Holler" in 1942. This is my favorite photo of her. Wasn't she beautiful at age 30?

Figure 10. Mom & her brother, Ken in 1913

Figure 11. Mom & her brother, Ken on the handcar. They rode it all around Redmon and he used to chew her out for not pedaling hard enough. Note the knickers. I wore those sometimes. From a postcard dated 1914.

Figure 12. My maternal grandparents, John, Jr. & Bertha Mason ("Me & Meme"), when they were newlyweds. Circa 1907.

Figure 13. My maternal grandfather, John Mason, Jr., age 30.

Figure 14. My paternal grandmother, Virginia Myers Hall ("Meme Hall"), age 20. Was that hat really in style in 1904?

Figure 15. My paternal grandfather, Thomas Eldridge Hall, age 25 (1907). He was always a hard worker.

Figure 16. Mom's girlhood home in Redmon, Illinois.
She used to go out on the porch roof and play.

Figure 17. House in Redmon showing bank building where failed robbery took place in 1907. Note the town's pump by the street. In the old days, there was a watering tank by the well where horses could drink.

Figure 18. My Grandfather Mason's first store and post office in Redmon, Illinois about 1905. He is second from left. Note the post office sign on the roof. This store burned down.

Figure 19. Second store-post office in Redmon. Note the dirt street and the wooden barrels. An early strip center.

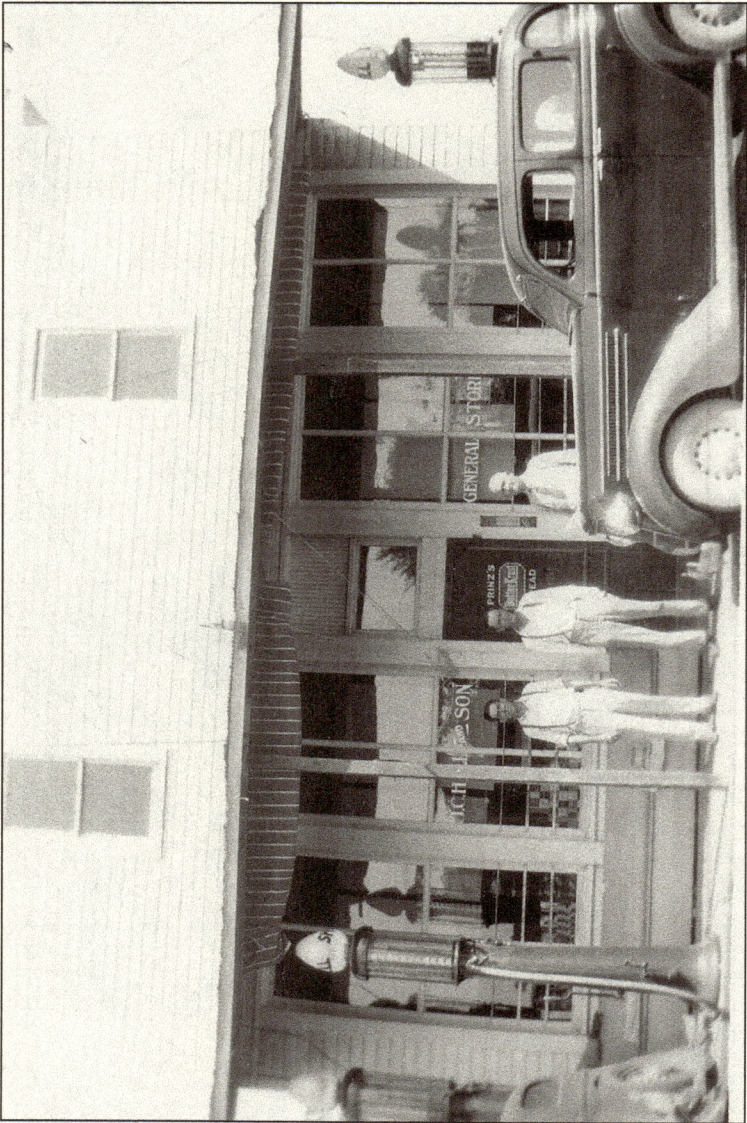

Figure 20. The "Big Store" in Leipsic, Indiana owned and operated by my maternal great grandfather, JC Hall. From left to right, Uncle Flet?, Uncle Harry Parish and JC.

Figure 21. JC Hall with one of the motor grocery stores or "huckster wagons." These carried a fairly complete inventory of essential grocery items.

Figure 22. The fleet of huckster wagons ("Flet's Fleet") parked beside the store in Leipsic with their respective drivers standing by.

Figure 23. My birthplace on West Crawford Street in Paris, Illinois. Mom and Dad first met in front of this house. We moved from here when I was very young.

Figure 24. My boyhood home in Northwest Paris. We lived here from about 1937 until we moved to the farm in 1948. My grandfather Mason's big garden was just to the right of the alley. They lived across the garden from us.

Figure 25. The outbuildings on Marion's farm northwest of Redmon, Illinois. Note the well next to the barnyard, not an ideal location for a water well. The double corn-crib is where his daughter, Pat, and I jumped into wag-onloads of grain.

Figure 26. Former bank building in Dana, Indiana that Dad and his father helped build. Note the well in the foreground where the well digger was almost killed due to a jammed winch.

Figure 27. The Island Queen unloading passengers in Cincinnati after they had a fun day at Coney Island Amusement Park. Circa 1940. Photo from the collection of the Public Library of Cincinnati & Hamilton County.

Figure 28. A customized 1937 Chrysler. This is similar to the one that served as our family car from 1937 until 1951 but ours did not have the alloy wheels. Note the "suicide" rear doors opening from front to rear. I hated this car when I was in senior high but have fond memories of it now. Photo courtesy of Ray McDonald.

Figure 29. A 1998 photo of Vance School in Paris, Illinois where Jody and I attended grades 1–6. The building no longer is used for a school and the tubular fire escape has been replaced with stairs.

Figure 30. The Edgar County Courthouse in Paris, Illinois. Note the automobiles of the period. From a penny postcard.

Chapter 7

Memory Nuggets From the Treasure Chest

Precious memories are a treasure.
We try our best to make them last

We keep them safely in our minds.
They are rich blessings from the past.
The Author

This chapter contains a collection of short stories that sometimes make their way through the misty fog of the past. Some of these make us chuckle, while others bring a tear to the eye, as we fondly remember the departed loved ones who touched our lives.

Scalp Fishing

Dad's brother, Jack, loved fishing as much as Dad did. While he was high school age, he and his friend Jim Martin, whose nickname was

"Slew Foot", went fishing one day at Twin Lakes. They were in Dad's boat going along the shore casting artificial lures, hoping for that big bass strike.

Jim got his lure caught in some weeds along the shore and gave the line a big jerk to try to free it. The lure came at him like a bullet and hit him on top of the head, imbedding two barbed prongs of a treble hook deep in his scalp. Jack assessed the situation and determined that it was hopeless to try to extract it there, so he cut the line and rowed the boat to the dock where they had left their bicycles.

They hurriedly jumped on their bikes and headed to Jack's house on North Street. Whenever there was a family emergency of any sort, Dad always seemed to be the one to call and this was no exception. Dad, Mom, Jody and I came out to the house to see what, if anything, could be done to help.

Dad sat Jim in a chair in the kitchen and looked at Jim's head. He thought he would be able to extract the hooks without too much trouble. He always kept the small blade of his pocketknife razor sharp so he was prepared. Mom stood by with the antiseptic and assisted the surgeon. My sister and I were observers. The thing about Dad was that he always seemed to know what he was doing, no matter what the situation, and this trait tended to give people around him a lot of confidence.

The first hook came out with not much of a problem, with no appreciable bloodshed. His assistant, Mom, kept it sponged up with a clean cloth. He had the second hook almost extracted but there was, what appeared to be, a tiny strip of flesh behind the barb. Dad cut the strip and the blood spurted; he had cut an artery, but the hook came out and poor Jim was free.

The blood spurted in rhythm to Jim's heartbeat and was coming out so profusely that it got ahead of Mom's sponging and began to run down the side of his head. After some quick thinking, she said, "Oops, I spilled this whole bottle of mercurochrome on his head."

Her remark avoided a panic and put Jim at ease. The blood flow was abated and Jim was as good as new. Mom should have been an OR assistant.

Jack said that the funny part of the story was, when they were on their bikes, the wind hitting the lure caused the spinner to spin rapidly enough to make a humming noise and they both laughed all the way to Jack's house.

Jim didn't tell his mom about the incident for fear that she wouldn't let him go fishing again. He just combed his hair over the wound and she never knew about it.

Bat Attack

According to a common theme in folklore about bats, people believe that they can become entangled in human hair, an unpleasant experience for women to say the least. According to popular belief, once a bat gets into a woman's hair, removing it is difficult. Some maintain that the bat will never let go, and that the woman must cut off her hair to get rid of it. Some believe that the bat will stay until driven out by thunder and lightning. Like snakes, women seem to have an inborn fear of them although they rarely become a victim of a bat in their hair. Bats are very complex creatures and know enough not to mess with women. Most men, including myself, could learn much from them.

Occasionally, but not too often, a bat got in our house. This always created quite a bit of excitement! The female residents usually beat a hasty retreat to the outside while Dad and I did something about the intruder. I always kind of enjoyed the chase. At first, we would try to capture them in a box or wastebasket, but their sonar was so efficient that they just darted away from a solid object coming at them. One time, Dad had so much trouble catching one that he threatened to resort to his shotgun, thinking the repair might be easier than trying to catch that darn bat. He gave up on this idea rather quickly.

Finally, we hit upon the idea of a tennis racquet and made an important discovery: their radar does not appear to be sensitive enough to detect the webbing in the racquet, so they would try to escape by flying through the middle. Sweet serendipity! However, the use of a tennis racquet took some practice in order to make its use practical. Once the bat was lodged against the webbing, one had to keep the racquet moving toward the side where the bat was trapped. If there were just an instant hesitation, the bat would fly away. I would sometimes wear my ball glove and clamp it over the bat on the racquet until I could take him outside and let him loose. By far the most effective tool was a fisherman's dip net, but sometimes it was difficult to round one up in a hurry.

Dad and I searched in vain to find their entryway into our living quarters. We assumed that they were coming down from the attic, so he plugged every opening from the attic to the outside and put fine screen wire over the vents. They still came!

One day I was at home with Mom and Jody, when a wandering bat made an appearance. I was enjoying watching it fly around, but all the screaming kind of got to me. They were yelling, "Danny, do something!" It was raining, so they didn't want to run outside. At one point, Jody thought sure that the bat had his sonar aimed at her hair, so she ran for her room and slammed the door shut. Mom and I could no longer see the bat and were afraid it had followed her through the door, but we heard no scream. Then we saw the bat caught between the door and the jamb in the upper corner of the door. That could never happen again in a hundred years!

Radio Racer

One day I was waiting for my newspapers to come off the press at the Beacon News and decided to go across the alley to browse at the Western Auto Store. I saw a portable radio that ran on batteries or you could plug it into a wall outlet. I decided to save my paper route money to buy it. I fancied having it up in my tree house, thinking it would be fun to listen to my favorite programs. I even thought I could strap it to my bike's crossbar and listen to it while I delivered my papers.

The day finally came when I had enough money, so I bought the radio and took it home to proudly show my family. For some reason, Dad did not like for me to have that radio. Maybe it was because I had not asked him for permission to buy it, or maybe it was because he thought I would get to be too worldly from listening to the music kids loved but parents hated. I didn't know why, and he would never tell me why. He just used that old saying, "A fool and his money are soon parted." I heard that phrase often while I was growing up, and even after I was an adult. I respected my father so I decided to return the radio.

I put the radio back in the box and took it back to the Western Auto Store. They told me I couldn't get cash back but could exchange it for something in the store. I looked around and finally saw a little red, gasoline powered racer that I kind of liked, but not as much as I liked the radio.

I would fire up the racer and hold it but didn't know how to control it and didn't want to just let it run free. I saw in the directions that you could attach it with a line to a pylon and it would run around in a circle. So, I drove a big nail into the center of the blacktop street in front of our house, and attached the racer to the nail with a heavy string fastened to an eye on the side of the racer. My friend directed traffic, what little there was, while I did my thing with the racer.

The racer started slowly around the "pylon" while spinning its wheels. The wheels gained traction and the car began to accelerate rapidly. It became just a red blur it was going so fast. There was so much centrifugal force that it broke the string and went lickety-split down the street. We heard the motor noise slowly fade then die in the distance. When we went looking for the racer, it was not to be found. I don't know if someone picked it up or if it ran under some bushes in a yard, but we looked and looked and never found it.

I wished I hadn't returned the radio.

Shoebox Streetcar

Even when I was a little kid, when I saw something that interested me, I tried to construct a model of it. I used cereal boxes, matchboxes, and other cardboard that I could find. I especially liked the cylindrical oatmeal boxes.

We rode on a streetcar in Terre Haute once, and I came home and built one out of a shoebox. It had windows covered with translucent tissue so that I could place a flashlight inside to light it up. I kept a collection of various size wheels that I had salvaged from torn-up toys. I confess that I had, on occasion, destroyed a toy I was tired of in order to use the wheels for another project of higher priority. Some of those toys would probably be worth some money nowadays. I watch the *Antiques Road Show* and it rankles me when I see a toy, exactly like one I had, that is now worth big money.

Once, after I had been to the farm and rode on the combine, I came home and made one that resembled the real thing. I even used an oatmeal box to construct a water tower for my electric train—no water, of course. That was the Lionel train that Mom had scrimped and saved out of her grocery money so she could get it for my Christmas. Sweet Mom! I had just completed the water tower when our dog, Topper, lifted his leg on it. I guess he wanted to be the one to provide the water. I could have killed him!

During the war, I made tanks, jeeps, ships, and more out of whatever I could find. Once I made a jeep from a kitchen matchbox but had run out of wheels. I found I could use the round seedpods from holly hawks. Those wheels would only last for a day because they dried and shriveled up, so frequent tire changes on the jeep were essential.

Jody and I sometimes made dolls from holly hawks. We used the blossoms for the skirts, buds for the heads and matchsticks for arms. We made men too, but I don't remember the method we used for them. The dolls also shriveled up overnight and turned from young people to old people. I know the feeling!

In that rich Illinois soil, dandelions grew tall and had thick, hollow stems. I used those stems for a lot of projects. I built little water towers by punching a hole near the bottom of an empty tin can, in which to fit the base of a large stem. I then perched the can on top of some sticks that formed the legs of the tower. I fitted stems together by putting the small ends into the large ends. I could deliver water for amazingly long distances with my dandelion stem pipeline. However, the water systems, like other projects made from vegetation, quickly dried up and became useless.

When I finally got an erector set (more scrimping), I was in heaven! I made all the projects in the instruction booklet and many, many more. I once saw a drilling rig and came home and made one. I had an electric motor and a gear box that I used to power my creations.

Everyone predicted I would grow up to be an engineer but, alas, I became a geologist because I was also interested in earth science. In my career, I got to be around drilling rigs, actually too much, and enjoyed being involved with other interesting oilfield equipment. I have never regretted the career I chose; it was good to my family for many years.

Water Magic

During the Pleistocene Era, four major ice sheets came down from the north and covered most of Northern and Central Illinois. One of these glaciers was named the Illinoian, which covered approximately 80% of the state. Beasts such as mastodons, saber-tooth cats, and long horn bison roamed the margins of these glaciers. When they melted, the glaciers left thick deposits of sand, silt, and gravel termed "glacial drift."

Years ago, the majority of farms in Northern and Central Illinois depended on water wells, hand dug through the glacial deposits to a maximum depth of 50 feet or so. These wells were shored up with metal hoops and wooden planks as digging progressed. If a good flow of water was observed, bricking up the walls would complete the well. These completed wells commonly had an internal diameter of three to four feet.

Whether or not a well could produce water was dependent upon whether the well bore intersected a bed or channel of sand and/or gravel, which could carry water to the well. It was not uncommon for a well to be dug through nothing but clay, which produced a dry well. Therefore, since it was expensive to dig a well, it was desirable for the well diggers to be able to determine whether or not the well would produce water or just result in a hole in the ground. No doubt you have heard the old saying, "He doesn't know his rear end from a hole in the ground!"

In an attempt to predict if a well would produce sufficient water, it was common for a well contractor to acquire the services of a diviner. The diviner would walk around with some kind of a device, but sometimes they just said they could envision water flowing underground. A device commonly used was a fork from a peach tree. They would hold the fork with a limb in each hand and, when they crossed a vein of water, the trunk of the fork would dip down. Sometimes they said they could even determine how deep it was to water. This practice was commonly called "water witching." The question often came up about payment for the diviner's services. Most of them would say that if they made it a practice to collect money, they would lose the gift of divining. I noticed, though, that most of them would accept gifts or favors.

One day, Dad came home and announced that his friend, Fred Powers, had a new well dug and it hit a really strong flow of water. He also said that the diviner left his peach fork there and, when Fred held it just right, he could walk up to the well and the trunk would dip down just like it did for the diviner.

Dad was overcome with curiosity so he took me out to Fred's farm to see if it worked for him. Dad held the fork just the way that Fred did and, sure enough, when he approached the well, it dipped. He did it time after time and it always worked. Once, he held the limbs so tightly that, when the trunk dipped, it twisted the bark right off the limbs. I finally got to try it and it worked for me. But the force was so strong it kind of scared me!

In my practice as a geologist, I witnessed diviners doing their thing many times. In the oil business, they called them "doodlebuggers" and many successful oil wells have been located according to the word of a diviner. Also, I have seen buried pipeline locations found with the use of two bent welding rods.

There has never been any scientific explanation for the success of divining, but I feel that it must work under certain conditions; however, I would never invest in an oil well with the location determined solely by a doodlebugger. I will never need to make that decision unless this book makes me a lot of money. If there were not something to it, then why is it mentioned in the Bible? Leviticus 19:26 states: "Do not practice divination or sorcery." We have all sinned!

Steamboat's a Comin'

Mom's brother, Ken Mason, and his family lived in Dayton, Ohio.

He was married to Doris and they had two sons, Mike and Phil. Mike was four years younger than me, and Phil was three years younger than Mike.

From time to time, we went to Dayton to visit them and we always had a grand time. Uncle Ken saw to that. He was so good with kids, and whenever we visited him or he came to visit, he always had a trinket for each of us kids.

I really liked playing with Mike, and when we managed to gather sufficient gas rationing coupons, we even visited them during the war. Mike and I always played soldier. He had an olive drab army guard belt that he wore constantly, and even slept with it on.

Ken usually took us to Cincinnati where we got on board the big steamboat, Island Queen, and rode up the Ohio River for about an hour to Coney Island amusement park. It was a case where the trip was as much fun as the destination for me, because I loved to study how that huge boat worked. I would go down to the first deck, and watch the big paddle wheels turn. Once, one of the crewmembers even took me on a tour of the engine room.

One time, when I was just a little guy, we arrived at the dock early and the Island Queen had not yet arrived. I was watching for it with great anticipation, and when I finally saw it coming, I shouted, "Steamboat's a comin'!" Everyone on the dock laughed.

Those trips were such fun even though we would be worn out by the time we got back to Dayton at the end of a long day. They almost shut the Island Queen down during the war, but the rationing board decided that it was such a morale booster during that trying time, that they would allocate sufficient fuel to keep it running.

In 1947, the boat went to Pittsburgh for a general overhaul. A welder's torch ignited a fuel tank and the Island Queen burned up or down, or whatever steamboats do when they catch fire. However, that grand old lady still plies the Ohio in my memory.

My brother, Gary, says he faintly remembers the Island Queen. He would have only been three years old when it made its last trip to Coney Island.

Uncle Ken's wife Doris died at an early age with breast cancer. She was such a pretty lady, inside and out, and had to leave two young sons. Phil was just a little guy, and when Doris found out that she was terminally ill, she wept whenever she realized that he would have little memory of her.

Uncle Ken finally remarried, but the love of his life was his "Dorie."

One Act Mess

In 1942, the Vance School PTA put on a play entitled *Henpecked Holler*. It was set in the mid nineteenth century and featured a bunch of ladies who liked to gossip. Mom was selected for a part in the play and we were all very proud of her. She was 30 years old and very beautiful in the old fashioned dress she wore for the play. There is a photo of her in that dress and it is my favorite of her (See photo section).

In our kitchen, we had a wooden, drop leaf table. We ate all of our meals on this table but it had a nasty habit. Once in a great while, one of the leaves would do a very nasty thing by dropping down at the worst possible moment. It happened so seldom that we tended to forget about it, and in doing so, we became vulnerable to its attacks. It had some kind of a collapsible metal device that served to hold the leaf in the up position and it must have been severely worn. I could never understand why my dad, who could do anything, didn't replace it or figure out another way to keep the leaf from collapsing. But, as I say, it happened so seldom that it kind of lulled you into thinking that it would never happen again.

On opening night of the play, everyone in the family was dressed in their best clothes and Dad even had on his one and only suit. He was so handsome when he had it on. We all sat down to supper and you can probably guess what happened next. Dad was sitting at the side with the tricky leaf and, sure enough, it decided that it would be a good time to do its thing.

The leaf came down and Dad jumped up! I made the mistake of laughing, which made matters worse. I bit my lip in a hurry. There he stood with a big gob of mashed potatoes right on his fly. A few peas were stuck to the right of the mashed potatoes and to the left; there was a big grease spot where the pork steak had impacted. He was a total mess and very mad! The only other time I saw him this mad was when he was wallpapering.

There wasn't much time to get Dad cleaned up but he and Mom did the best they could to get all the food stains off his pants. Poor Mom and poor Dad! What a thing to have happen just before she had to perform in the play. The last I remember about the soiled pants incident was them hanging on a chair with the electric fan aimed at them in an attempt to get them dry. They must have been sufficiently dry for him to put them back on, because he wore them to the play that evening. I imagine they were still damp.

The play came off without a hitch and Mom played her part flaw-lessly.

Frosty Mornings

Our milk was delivered to the porch very early every morning in returnable glass bottles. It was before milk was homogenized, so the cream would rise to the top until you shook the bottle. On a really cold winter morning, I liked to bring the milk in from outside. Those were about the only mornings I didn't fuss about getting out of bed. On those mornings, I would find columns of frozen cream pushing up from the top of the bottles with the cardboard lids perched on top. I would take the bottles to the kitchen and slice off the columns of cream, which could be two or more inches in height, and eat them. I usually had to share with my sister. Mom hated for us to do this because it made the milk thin, kind of like the one percent milk we buy today. I miss the milk bottles with the cream on top!

There was usually at least one winter morning when you went to school and saw a kid with his tongue stuck to the flagpole. You could sometimes get a new sucker to take the dare and stick his tongue on the cold metal. You would think that you could just touch the tip to it instantly and it wouldn't freeze in place. That maneuver sometimes worked and you could win the dare, but, if it was cold enough, it stuck. The other kids would be standing around the flagpole laughing at the victim until a teacher came out with a container of warm water to pour on the unfortunate tongue. If you tried to pull your tongue away too fast, you would leave a little bit of meat on the pole. How do I know this?

Square Parking

Paris, Illinois is the county seat of Edgar County and has a courthouse and a town square with stores, shops and a movie theater around the square, all facing the courthouse. When I was a kid, Saturday was the big night downtown and the stores were all open late. There was usually a band concert held in a bandstand on the courthouse lawn. Popcorn was sold from a wagon that looked something like a stagecoach. It could be a scene right out of Mayberry, USA, and the place to be on Saturday night.

Dad would drive us downtown on a Saturday evening and park

along the street facing the storefronts. A favorite place to park was near the Lincoln Theater because there was usually a lot of activity along the sidewalk there, especially when the show let out. We would just sit in the car, watch the people walk by and listen to the band. Mom and Dad sometimes waved to people they knew and some of the folks came up to the car to chat awhile. There were often remarks made about the people they observed, such as: he or she is looking older, gaining weight, looks pregnant, is with a partner not their spouse, etc., etc. It was so bad that when Jody got older, she hated to get out of the car for fear she would be discussed.

That square parking seems sort of kooky nowadays but it was a popular activity back then when money was not too plentiful. Even so, Dad would sometimes buy us a sack of popcorn or a Hershey bar if we had been good. I still like Hershey bars because they bring back memories of my father.

This n' That

Beat it, Kid! There was a tradition of thoroughly cleaning house in the spring and fall. The floor cleaning tools consisted of a broom, dust mop, and maybe a carpet sweeper. If you were better off, you could afford a Hoover vacuum cleaner, but these were hard to come by during the war.

Wall to wall carpeting had not yet come into vogue, so area rugs warmed the floors. Wool, jute-backed rugs could collect an amazing amount of dust over a six-month period. The most efficient method of cleaning them meant you had to take them outside, hang them over a clothesline and use a wire rug beater to beat the devil out of them. This job often fell to kids with the instructions to whup up on the rug until no more dust came out of it.

If you set about to beat *all* the dust out of a 9'x 12' rug, you had quite a job on your hands! At first it was great fun. There was the simple forehand stroke, the backhand, the over the shoulder, between the legs, etc. One could be very creative with this, but it really got to be a drag before the job was complete. If a neighborhood kid walked by and saw you taking your frustrations out on a poor, defenseless rug, it was almost impossible for them to pass by without asking you to let them have a few whacks at it. It was kind of like Tom Sawyer whitewashing the fence, because one could make the most out of a bad situation. I once traded 100 whacks for three aggie marbles. An opportunity must be taken advantage of when it presents itself.

Riding the Bars. It was a common practice in those days to give another kid a ride on your handlebars. Of course safety helmets were unknown and we couldn't have afforded them anyway. When my brother Gary was old enough, I used to take him places by giving him a ride on my bike. He would perch there with his feet on the front fender and his hands gripping the bars just in front of mine. We never had an accident but one time a dog ran in front of us and it was a close call.

I loved to take him to Carli's store on Vance Street where they had such neat stuff for kids. After I had my paper route, I could afford to buy us candy and knick-knacks. It was fun to take him in the store because he was such a cute little kid that people noticed him. It was a good way to meet new girls in the neighborhood since they never seemed to resist bending down to talk to him. Then I could pick up on the conversation.

A Tisket, A Tasket, a pretty May basket! In our town, it was a custom to make May baskets to hang on the doorknobs the night before May Day. My sister and I would work for days making the little baskets out of wallpaper samples. We had about five or six different designs, and I can still remember how to make them. Then we went out and picked wild flowers such as violets and dandelions to put in them, along with a piece or two of hard candy. We had them all prepared before the sun went down on April 30. Then we would go out and hang them on neighbor's doors after dark. That was such a sweet thing for kids to do. I wonder if they still do it anywhere in the world. (I once made a kind of nasty May basket for a teacher I didn't like, but I won't go there now.)

The Iceman Cometh. When we lived in Paris, it was still common to get ice delivered to your house. Although most people had refrigerators by then, you sometimes needed ice for other purposes, such as making home made ice cream. When it was really, really hot, you could place a big hunk of ice in a tub in front of the electric fan and it would cool down a room. That was a rare treat.

When you needed an ice delivery, you put a card with a big number in a front window. When the iceman saw the card with a 25, for instance, he would stop his truck, put a rubber cape over his shoulders to keep himself dry, and bring a 25-pound chunk of ice to your door, carrying it over his shoulder with ice tongs. He would then put the ice in your icebox if you had one. On hot summer days, we loved to meet him at his truck where he would give us each a small sliver of ice to suck on, a special summer treat.

Tin Can Stilts. We discovered that if you laid a tin can, with just holes punched in one end, and the other end still solid, on its side and stomped on it, the ends would curl up around the edges of your soles and stick to your shoes. Then you could walk around making a lot of noise, especially on pavement. The more noise, the better!

And, speaking of stilts, the girls across the street showed up one day with wooden stilts that their daddy had made for them. I was very jealous, so when Dad came home, I told him that their daddy had made them a pair of stilts. In about a day or so, he made us a pair that was even better than theirs. He took the bait, hook, line and sinker!

Motorcycle Dreamin'. Then there was the ever-popular activity of fastening a playing card to a fender brace on your bicycle with a clothespin, so that the spokes would flip it. We all thought it would then sound kind of like a motorcycle. If you used two cards, we imagined it sounded like a powerful twin cylinder motorcycle. Kids had to have a vivid imagination in those days to keep from going nuts from boredom.

Marked Houses. In the days following the great depression, there were still a number of tramps wandering about in our town. Paris was a railroad town, so many of them came to town riding the trains. It was a known fact that they would mark houses where they could get food handouts. These marks were distinguishable only to other tramps or hobos. Dad's parents, on North Street, had such a mark and, although we looked and looked, we could never find it. They always had a big garden and would share their food with the tramps that stopped by. A few of them insisted on doing some chores to pay for the food, so my grandfather, Tom, always kept a few jobs, such as mowing the lawn, for them to do. Even then, I respected the ones who wanted to help their benefactors and suspected that they were the first ones to get steady jobs when the economy improved.

Bug Lamps. On a summer evening in Illinois, the air would be filled with fireflies or lightning bugs as we called them. It was fun to catch them and watch their little tails light up. Sometimes we would punch small holes in the lids of fruit jars, put a number of them in the jar and use it for a lantern. I would keep it next to my bed and it would produce a soft glow. However, I usually went out on the front porch and removed the lid before I went to sleep. There was no joy in waking the next morning to find a jar full of dead bugs.

Captain Drake. My sister loved to play paper dolls and liked for me to role-play with her. She liked to assume the character of Brenda Star, a reporter for a large metropolitan newspaper. She had quite a collection of paper clothing for her little paper doll and she was very creative in dressing her with accessories and all. I thought it was kind of silly but I went along with her. I balked, though, at playing the part of a woman. One of the parts I didn't mind playing was that of Captain Drake, a swashbuckling sea captain who was always rescuing damsels in distress. We had an old cast iron ship that used to be a lamp but was then used as a doorstop. I would put Captain Drake on it and he could "sail" all over the house saving one woman after another. I still have that old ship and it is now an antique. I made the mistake of repainting it, which destroyed a lot of its value.

Playin' the Bones.   My grandfather, Me Mason, was said to be quite a musician when he was young. When I was just a little tyke, he would get me on his lap and we would play like we were in a band. He must have played a trombone, because he usually mimicked the movement of the slide and the sound. I played the drums, or a trumpet, or whatever instrument I was assigned. Sometimes he would even let me play his imaginary trombone. How I would love to sit on his lap and play in his band just once more. Maybe in the sweet by and by!

He had a set of rib bones that he used to play rhythm with, and he was quite good with them. Does anyone ever play bones nowadays?

Chapter 8

Old Tales We Loved to Hear

Old tales our loving parents told,
Passed on to us from days of old.

Precious stories from days gone by,
Shall we pass them on or let them die?

Memories are a special gift.
We love the pleasant kind.

The treasure our children will value most,
When we leave this world behind.
The Author

This chapter contains a collection of stories we heard our parents and grandparents tell from time to time. They must have been true because more than one person told some of them and they were always the same. Is that the test for truth?

The Redmon Fire

My great grandmother Caroline Mason had arthritis, and the pain commonly interfered with her sleep. One winter night she noticed a glow at the elevator across the street from their house and saw that it was on fire. She woke the family and my grandfather, John Mason, Jr., threw his coat over his pajamas and ran out to ring the fire bell, which was used to summon the volunteer firemen. He was in such haste that he forgot to put his shoes on. His mother saw him out there barefooted and ran out to place his shoes beside him. He didn't stop ringing the bell long enough to put them on.

I don't know how much damage was done to the elevator, but he was kind of a hero in town for a while. More than one person came into his drug store with this question: "Johnny, why did you take off your shoes before you rang the fire bell?"

The Failed Bank Robbery

In 1907, there was an attempt to rob the Redmon bank. The robber was trying to pry open a window on the west side of the building. There is some controversy over what happened next, but someone in the bank heard him trying to gain entrance. Who that someone was, remains unknown. Some reports state that it was the owner of the bank, while others say it was the night watchman. To my knowledge, no one ever admitted to taking part in what happened next.

The person in the bank quietly made his way to the window on the second story, directly above where the prying was taking place. Each time the would-be robber pried, the window above was opened just a bit. The opening was timed to correlate exactly with the noise the robber made. When the window was opened enough, the person stuck his pistol out the window and fired three shots straight down without viewing his target. Two of the bullets found their mark while the third glanced off the robber's skull.

The robber fell mortally wounded and my grandparents, who lived about 200 feet west of the bank, and other town folk heard him groaning until daylight, when he was found dead. Everyone was afraid to help him for fear he was armed or his buddies were nearby.

The identity of the robber was never known. However, it was said that he had silk underwear, which in those days signified wealth. He also had sufficient nitro glycerin and blasting caps to allow him to blow the bank vault. He was buried in an unmarked grave at Embarrass Cemetery.

Storybook Romance

My grandfather, John Mason, Jr. ("Me Mason") was a lonely bachelor of 34 living in the tiny town of Redmon, Illinois where he was the proprietor of a drug store and post office. There were no young girls around Redmon that captured his interest, which was very frustrating for him. In those days, it was difficult to travel to a larger town, such as Paris, just to search for romance.

To pass the time, he would scan the lonely-hearts ads in the magazines that came through the post office. He finally ran an ad, which resulted in a reply. So, he began to write to Bertha Hall who was a schoolteacher in French Lick, Indiana. She was 13 years younger than him. Remember that my mother married my dad who was also a Hall, lest you be confused.

The following excerpt is from a letter he wrote to Bertha while he was running for the office of Village Treasurer.

Old Tales We Loved to Hear

Redmon, Ill.
March 26, 1906

Miss Bertha B. Hall
French Lick, Ind.

Dear Bertha:

If I am elected this time, I will use some of my money to visit my sweet little girl in F.L. Now don't get mad when I call you sweet for your picture shows plainly that you are and I am coming over soon to see if your picture tells me the truth. I get your picture out nearly every day and take a good look at it. And I think of you too every day and wish that I was down there if it was only for an hour. Now Bertha when I do come to see you I'm going to kiss you right dab slap in the mouth. So you can prepare for it.

Do you think I would go over a hundred miles to see a girl as sweet as you look and then never kiss her? Well I guess not, and if you get off with less than a hundred you will do well. I'm a Kisser from Kisserville when I get started. That's one reason I never got married. I's always afraid I'd kiss my wife to death. How is your constitution, Bertha, is it all OK?

Well, I will close my letter. Now write soon and don't wait as long as I did. Don't forget to 'fodder the hosses' and 'kiss the kids.'

From your lover,
John

To tell the truth, I feel a little guilty for invading my grandparents' privacy by passing along this letter, but after more than 100 years, I thought it would be OK.

When he told her to "fodder the hosses," remember that she drove to school in her buggy every day, and his phrase, "kiss the kids" no doubt referred to the kids in her class.

Well, he did take the train to French Lick and was pleased with the young lady he met there. They were married on May 8, 1907, the same week my dad was born.

I have related what little I know about their courtship, but I would venture to say that they both came to marriage chaste. That was more common than not in those days. Since the advent of the pill, and the sexual revolution in the 1960s and 70s, the situation has more or less reversed. I can only say that more marriages lasted a lifetime and commitments were generally taken more seriously in those times.

Chastity for single women was considered a treasure that was closely guarded by their families. If you tour a home from the 19th century with the original furniture, you will often see a bundling bed. This was a full size bed with provision for a wide board to be placed down the center. When a young man came a long way on horseback or by buggy to court the daughter, it was often too far for him to return home on the same evening. They would bundle the couple tightly in bedclothes and, since beds were at a premium in a small home, they would allow them to both sleep in the bed with the board down the middle to keep them apart. I imagine that they could expect the father or mother to walk in to check on them at any time.

Have our social mores changed much over the years?

John and Bertha Mason had two children: Ken, who was born in 1908, and my mother, Edna, who was born in 1912, the same year as the sinking of the Titanic.

Practical Jokes

My grandfather loved gadgets and anything that had to do with playing a joke on somebody. When he and Bertha were first married, they looked through novelty catalogs and often ordered funny items. They once got a big wind-up bug that would flap its wings and make a buzzing sound as it ran across the floor.

They were both laid up with the flu one winter and had to have their groceries delivered to their house. This is the house where Uncle Ken and my mother were born, but it is no longer standing. The man who delivered their groceries was scared to death he would get the flu so he just put the sacks of groceries on the edge of the porch. One day, when he made his delivery, my grandfather released the bug to run at him and said, "Look out, this flu bug will get you!"

The drugstore/post office in Redmon had benches where the locals could relax and take in the goings on in the town. When my grandfather was the proprietor, he rigged up a little paddle on a hinge under a bench. The end of the paddle opposite the hinge had a small peg that was positioned below a tiny hole in the seat of the bench. Then he had a string attached to the paddle, which, when pulled, would cause the peg to pop up through the hole. The string was concealed and ran to a point near the cash register.

When my grandfather saw someone sitting on the exact spot above the peg, he would yank the string. The peg would pop up and the victim would pop up. They would turn around to inspect the seat but not find the peg because the spring on the paddle had already pulled it back down through the hole. The benches were fastened down to the floor and enclosed around the sides so that the mechanism of the butt poker could not be discovered. It's a wonder my grandfather had any customers but I guess they were all used to him. He had plenty of jokes played on him as well.

At the back of his store, there was a potbelly stove where the men would pull up their chairs and tell tall tales when it was too cold to be outside. I can imagine it got pretty deep in there.

Some evenings it was difficult to get the loafers to leave so that my grandfather could close his store. He would open a bottle of ammonia and set it near the bunch of guys. After a while, they would pull their handkerchiefs out and begin wiping their eyes. This tear gas trick usually worked to break up the group.

One evening, someone opened the door of the stove and threw in a handful of .22 short cartridges. In just a little while, they began cooking off with much noise and the men scattered like quail. It knocked the stovepipe loose from the flue opening and the soot flew everywhere. The walls of the stove were too thick for anything to penetrate them, but the popping sure got everyone's attention. I would say my grandfather deserved that little caper. I don't know if he ever discovered who the prankster was.

The Entertainers

When my mother and Uncle Ken were kids, they were so cute together that they were often invited to sing and perform skits at church and school functions as well as at other community meetings. Remember that he was four years older than her. One of the songs they sang went something like this:

<u>Who Stole the Lock on the Henhouse Door</u>

Who stole the lock? – I don't know.
Who stole the lock on the henhouse door?
I'll find out afore I go,
Who stole the lock on the henhouse door.

Down in the henhouse on my knees.
I thought I heard a chicken sneeze.

'Twas only ole rooster sayin' his prayers.
And passing out hymns to the hens upstairs.

Who stole the lock? – I don't know.
Who stole the lock on the henhouse door?
I'll find out afore I go,
Who stole the lock on the henhouse door.

Fire in the Hole

When Dad was in his late teens, he worked with his dad, Tom, on construction projects. Tom was a contractor involved in building a bank in Dana, Indiana where they were digging a well for the bank. They all sat down under a tree to have lunch one day when the well digger came up and asked for a favor. He wanted to set off a charge of dynamite in the bottom of the well to make it easier to dig. He intended to set it off before he ate lunch so that the nitrate fumes would dissipate before he had to go back into the well. He wanted someone to lower him into the well and to winch him up after he lit the fuse. Dad volunteered.

Dad lowered him into the well without any problem and the fuse was lit. Then the man yelled, "Now get me out of here fast!" Dad had just started to winch him up when his pant leg got wound up in the gears of the winch and he could get him no higher than just a few feet off bottom. The man in the well started screaming to get him out because it would be sure death if he were left there when the charge went off.

A burley man, eating lunch, heard the screaming and ran over to the winch to help out. His strength was no doubt aided by adrenalin. He had to lower the man back down the well a little bit to free the cloth from the gears. Can you imagine what the well digger thought when he found himself being lowered back down on top of the charge? He was then winched out of the well as rapidly as he could be. As soon as the bucket reached the top, the digger jumped out just as the charge went off. A close call indeed!

The Big Move

In 1920, when my mother was eight years old and her brother, Ken was twelve, the family moved from the house in Redmon to the house on West Crawford Street in Paris. My great grandfather, John Mason, Sr., lived with them, his wife Caroline having passed in 1914. One of the reasons for the move was that my grandmother, Meme Mason, wanted to live in a larger town than Redmon. Also, Grandfather Mason was 80 and they felt that he needed to be close to better medical facilities.

That is where my mother lived when she met my dad and where Jody and I were born.

When my grandfather moved to Paris, he became the proprietor of a small grocery store on the west side of town across from the cereal mill on Jefferson Street. At one time, he also sold Bibles and other Christian books door to door. My mother once looked at the logbook of his house calls and sales and noticed that some of the ladies had the notation, "HC," penciled in after their names. She finally persuaded her dad to tell her that it stood for "Hell Cat."

He often found himself on the street after dark when he was walking home from the store or his book selling. He commonly had to carry quite a sum of money on his person and believed he would probably be held up sometime. He always kept the money in his right pants pocket in a roll that was secured with a rubber band and walked with his hands in his pockets. He thought that if he was held up, he could flip the roll behind him when he drew his hands out of his pockets. He practiced his move in front of a mirror and became pretty slick at it, making it one smooth motion with the flip not noticeable.

One night, he met a shady looking guy on the street and thought he would be held up so he did his money flip. The guy walked on by and my grandfather turned around to retrieve his money roll. It wasn't there! He looked and looked to no avail, went home to get a flashlight, came back and looked some more. He never did find it and when he would pass that spot years later, he would stop to look for his money. Like I said, he was a character!

Visiting Pastors and Musical Chairs

My grandparents, Meme and Me Mason, often invited visiting pastors over to their house for a meal after church on Sundays. My grandfather kept an old wooden chair in the basement by the furnace, where he would sit and chew tobacco while he was tending the furnace and doing other basement chores. The old chair had a wide crack down the middle of the seat that would pinch the sitter's bottom if he were not careful. He always took care to get his crack lined up with the crack in the chair so as not to get a good pinch.

One Sunday, the visiting preacher came down the basement to see him and plopped down in the chair. He let out a yell that could probably have been heard a block away. Meme rushed down to the basement to see what in the world had happened. There stood the pastor rubbing his butt and pointing at the chair.

When they still lived in Redmon, a pastor was visiting one Sunday afternoon, when Uncle Ken, who was just a little tyke, threw a rock and killed a little chicken. He felt so badly about it that he was sobbing when his mother came out to comfort him. She was asking him why he threw the rock at the poor little chicken and if he was sorry he killed it. He said through his sobs, "I didn't mean

154

to. I was aiming at the preacher."

When my mother was a little girl, she was coached to always take the neck or gizzard when fried chicken was being served to a visiting pastor so that he could have enough of the choice pieces. I guess all preachers loved fried chicken, so the story goes. When she was an adult having company, she still always took the neck or gizzard, claiming that she had acquired a fondness for them when she was a child. Maybe so, but I think she just wanted to make sure everyone else had the best pieces. She was so unselfish!

Once my grandfather noticed that the rear leg on a chair was in need of repair and told the members of his family not to sit in it until he could get it fixed. Later on, they were all sitting in the living room when he came in to sit with them. They heard a crash, looked over, and saw his feet sticking up in the air. He had forgotten about the chair with the bad leg and sat down in it.

Off to College

Mom's brother, Ken, graduated from Paris High School in about 1926 and wanted to go to college. He went to Indiana Central for a short time to complete some basic courses and then decided he wanted to go to the University of Illinois.

Before he left for Champaign-Urbana, he and his father sat down and determined how much it would cost for his room, board, spending money, books and tuition for the first year. Then his father deposited that sum of money in a bank in Champaign for Ken to draw from.

He started at U of I in the fall and everything went according to the plan. Then sometime during the spring semester, his parents received a post card from New York City. Ken and his friend had bought motorcycles and were having fun in the big city. You can only imagine how this news affected his parents! He stayed there for about three months, just having fun until his money ran out.

Well, my Uncle Ken finally came home and his father told him that there would be no more money for college. I don't know if he was able to keep his bike.

Ken went to work at U.O.Colson Company in the advertising business and completed about two years' credit by taking correspondence courses. He spent his entire career in the advertising and printing industry, employed for a long time at Reynolds and Reynolds Company in Dayton, Ohio, then eventually partnering with a friend to open their own business in Denver. That venture did not end well.

The Old Pickup Line

One evening in 1928 or so, Dad was driving with a friend, Paul V., in the delivery truck provided by the grocery store where he worked. They saw a big Hudson automobile go by and Dad said to his friend, "Did you see what I saw?" Paul replied, "You mean that pretty girl driving that car?" Dad said, "Yes, and I'm going to marry her!"

Dad ditched his friend as quickly as he could and began searching the streets of Paris looking for the Hudson. He remembered that it had a decal from the University of Illinois in the back window so he naturally thought the driver was a coed there. Actually, it was Mom's brother Ken who was going to U of I.

Dad finally found the car parked in front of the house on Crawford Street where my mother was sitting out front, waiting for her mother to come out of the house so she could drive her somewhere. Dad stopped and said to Mom, "Haven't I met you somewhere before?" She replied that she didn't think so, but the ice was broken. You would think that Dad could have come up with a more original line to pick up such a classy gal.

Dad cut a pretty dashing figure when he was a young guy, and a whirlwind romance culminated in their marriage when Mom was only 16 and Dad was 21. Dad reminded my mom's mother of a drummer who came through French Lick when she was teaching there. She had a crush on him but he moved on before it had a chance to blossom. She still fondly remembered him, and that must have influenced her somewhat when she encouraged Mom to marry Dad.

Sneaky Thief

After the move from Redmon to Paris, my grandfather Mason ran the store on Jefferson Street by the cereal mill. He kept saying that he thought he was missing inventory on a continuing basis, but everyone thought he was just losing count of stuff. So, when he left the store one evening, he used two hunks of chewing gum to secure a short length of string across the top of the front door then exited through the side door. Sure enough, the next morning the telltale string was hanging down, indicating that the door had been opened. He did this every night for a while and every morning it showed the door had been opened. Finally, his family believed him.

Dad and Mom were married then, and living with her folks on Crawford Street. Dad volunteered to set a trap for the thief, and Mom insisted on going with him. So, one night they took a pistol to the store to lie in wait for the thief. The plan was to wait inside in the dark until he got all the way inside, then turn on the light and hold him at gunpoint while they called the police.

They waited and waited inside the store with the lights out for what seemed like an eternity. Sure enough, about 1:00 AM, they heard footsteps coming across the wooden porch. Then they heard a key being turned in the lock and the door opening. They waited for what they thought was an appropriate length of time for the door to be closed behind the intruder; then they jumped up, turned on the light and shouted, "Halt!" However, they acted too quickly, for the door was still open behind the thief and he fled through it.

They got a good look at the man's face, though, and saw that he was the guy who lived next to the store. That ended the thefts, so one might say that the operation was a failure but the result was a success, the opposite of the usual saying.

Wise Sayings

The following is a collection of popular sayings of the times. Some of these we heard so often that we got sick of them.

> *"A fool and his money are soon parted."* Dad's all time favorite.

> *"What you don't have in your head, you have to have in your heels."* Indicates that if you forget something, you must go get it, one of Mom's favorites.

> *"As long as you put your feet under my table, you must obey the rules."* Another of Dad's favorites that ranks right up there with the first one.

> *"Give it a lick and a promise."* To make quick work of it, one of Mom's favorites.

> *"Fiddle sticks!"* As close as Mom got to swearing.

> *"Rattle brain."* I often was called that.

> *"Flash in the pan."* What Dad often called my sister, Jody.

"Living high on the hog." Extravagant life style. We never had that problem.

"Drunker than a skunk." We never did that either.

"Cock and bull story." Often shared among friends for entertainment.

"Don't count your chickens before they hatch." I'm not counting the money from this book selling.....yet!

"How's your copperosity?" Meaning your general sense of well-being. Dad often said this but I have only heard one other person say it.

"You shoot like an old wash woman." Another of Dad's favorites to say when someone shot poorly.

"Worthless as tits on a boar." I sometimes heard this when I did a poor job on something.

"Still wet behind the ears." A newbie.

"You're a pantywaist." A "chicken."

"Deadbeat." Didn't pay their debts. Dad really looked down on those folks.

"Going to hell in a hand basket." In bad shape.

"Conniption fit." We hated to see one of those!

"Not worth a hill o' beans." Have you checked the price of soybeans lately? That hill could be worth a fortune!

"Shooting the bull." Telling stories.

"Beating around the bush." Being evasive. Politicians often do it.

"Passing the buck." Blaming someone else. Politicians are experts at this.

"Making mountains out of molehills." Much ado about nothing.

"Hitting the nail on the head." Being right about something. Like when you say politicians pass the buck and beat around the bush.

"Burning your candle at both ends." Trying to do too much.

"You've got your dander up." Mad as a wet hen. Cats also get about that mad when they get wet. How do I know this?

"She's a humdinger." Something to behold. Can have a multitude of applications.

"This neck of the woods." Around here.

"Knocking on wood." Keep it from happening.

"Big wig." Important person or one who thinks he is.

"Running off at the mouth." Talking too much. Another thing politicians do.

"Blabber mouth." See above.

"Just consider the source." Take with a grain of salt.

"Birds of a feather flock together." You will be judged

by the company you keep. Be careful!

"Tight as a new boot." One who hates to spend money.

"Stubborn as a mule." Uncooperative person.

"Higher than a kite." Prices nowadays.

"Holy Terror." Used many ways.

"Warm as toast." Comfortable.

"Rule of thumb." A well known method.

"Sticks in my craw." Difficult to accept.

"Belly ache." Complain.

"Fly off the handle." Get mad. Sometimes like a wet hen.

"On pins and needles." Anticipation until something happens, often something undesirable.

"Smart aleck." Annoying person.

"As honest as the day is long." Trustworthy. All politicians claim this quality. (Can you tell this is an election year?)

"Did himself in." Worked too hard.

"Can't see the forest for the trees." Don't understand though it is apparent.

"Goody two shoes." A persnickety person.

"Tan your hide." Give you a spanking.

"Nail you to the big barn door." Beat you at something.

"Lock, stock and barrel." The whole thing.

"You don't have a leg to stand on." Not much evidence.

"Raining cats and dogs." Really coming down.

"Blind as a bat." Difficulty understanding. But bats aren't really blind.

"Strong as an ox." Are they that strong?

"Sicker than a dog." Dogs must really get sick.

"Wise as an owl." Are they really wise?

"Crooked as a dog's hind leg." Can be used literally or to describe a dishonest person.

"Looked sheepish." A guilty look.

"Poor as a church mouse." We weren't quite that poor.

"Quicker than lightning." That's quick!

"Love is blind." Jody and I were often told this about our romantic relationships.

"Don't take any wooden nickels." Don't be fooled.

"Don't poke a hornet's nest." Don't stir up trouble.

"let sleeping dogs lie." See above.

"Blown to smithereens." Something gone bad.

"Went like a house on fire." But not as quick as lightning.

"King pin." The person in charge.

"Chief cook and bottle washer." Derogatory term for person in charge.

"Your goose is cooked." Caught!

"Buy a pig in a poke." Unseen purchase.

"Bury the hatchet." Make peace.

"Go off half cocked." Not prepared.

"Tied to mother's apron strings." Sheltered.

"Eat crow." Apologize.

"Cut the mustard." Get er' done.

"Pay the fiddler (or piper)." Not much is free.

"Don't cry over spilt milk." Let it go.

"Fly-by-night." Questionable person or practice.

"Throw a monkey wrench in something." Mess it up.

"Go hog wild." Craziness

"A bone to pick with someone." A serious discussion.

"Lollygagging." Being lazy.

"He doesn't have a lick of sense." Stupid.

"Tolerable." Acceptable.

"Put the kibash to it." Kill it.

"I reckon." I guess.

"The whole kit and caboodle." All of it. Lock, stock and barrel.

"Crazy as a bedbug." Why are they crazy?

"Crazy like a fox." Very cunning.

"Worked like a dog." Is that why they get so sick?

"Spill the beans." Tell a secret.

"To beat the band." To do with vigor.

"More than one way to skin a cat." Several ways to do something.

"Hold your horses." Wait.

"Making a silk purse out of a sow's ear." Making something valuable from something worthless.

"Keep your shirt on." Be patient. (What you must do to read all these sayings!)

Chapter 9

Good News

"The Lord is my shepherd;
I shall not want.

He maketh me to lie down in
green pastures: He leadeth me
beside the still waters.

He restoreth my soul: He leadeth me
in the paths of righteousness
for His name's sake.

Yea, though I walk through
the valley of the shadow of death,
I will fear no evil: for Thou art
with me; Thy rod and Thy staff
they comfort me.

Thou preparest a table before
me in the presence of mine enemies:
Thou anointest my head
with oil; my cup runneth over.

Surely goodness and mercy
shall follow me all the days of my life:
and I will dwell in the house of the Lord
forever. "

Psalm 23 (KJV)

I n the mid Nineteenth Century, there was a peasant family with a young daughter living near Wurtemberg, Germany. They heard stories about the new world and how wonderful it must be to live where you had religious freedom and could acquire rich farmland, which, compared to their homeland, was plentiful. So, they saved their money to make their dreams come true.

They finally saved enough money and prayed for God's protection and mercy as they prepared for their long, treacherous journey to America. It was 1852 and their little daughter, Caroline, was now seven years old, and strong enough to make the journey.

They packed all their earthly belongings in a wagon and headed for the seaport in Hamburg. This stage of their trip took the most part of a week. There, they sold their horses and wagon and booked passage on a sailing ship bound for the new world.

The trip across the open ocean for weeks took its toll. There was sickness on board that resulted in several deaths. Those who died were buried at sea. But the little family from Wurtemberg survived the trip.

They arrived in New York where they purchased a covered wagon and a team of horses and headed west, because they heard that America's heartland had rich soil and a climate well suited for farming. In 1853, they finally settled near Oakland, Illinois and thanked the good Lord for his protection.

The above narrative may not be accurate in every detail, but the actual journey must have been very similar to the above description. I obtained the information from Mom, other relatives, and a friend who is familiar with the history of Germany in the Nineteenth Century.

That family was John and Christina Gritz, and their daughter Caroline was my great grandmother. My great grandfather, John Mason Sr., often traveled from Redmon to Oakland on business and met Caroline there. In 1866 they were married and settled in Redmon. Their marriage produced a son, John, Jr. (Me Mason) and a daughter, Annie. An infant son died shortly after birth. All of these folks are buried at Embarrass Cemetery, west of Redmon.

My father was also blessed with Christian ancestors. His grandfather, Wesley Marcelus Hall, was ordained in the Methodist Church in 1898.

The reason I emphasize this part of my families' history is because it is an important part of my Christian heritage for which I am thankful. My wife, Twila, also has a strong Christian heritage.

At Mother's Knee

Some of my earliest childhood memories involve attending church and Sunday school at the First Baptist Church in Paris, Illinois. I wish I could remember my Sunday school teacher's name because she was much more than just a baby sitter. She taught us Bible verses and told us Bible stories. We made simple craft projects such as a cross made from Popsicle sticks, little lambs made from cotton, a shepherd's crook from a tree limb, etc.

I must have been really young when Mom began reading to me from an orange Bible storybook. It had line drawings illustrating the stories and I would sit for hours studying the drawings in that old book. I wish I had that book.

One day, when I must have been five or so, Mom told me that I was reaching the age of accountability and that I had to make a decision about whether to accept Jesus as my savior. I told her that I loved Jesus and couldn't understand why it was so necessary to take this step. Well, she spent considerable time over the next several days explaining the plan of salvation to me.

She explained that Jesus was God's only son who was sent to earth to be sacrificed for mankind's sins and that a person had to confess his sins, ask for forgiveness and accept Jesus into his heart as his personal savior. She said that once you did this with sincerity, you would go to heaven. Of course, I wanted to go to heaven but not right away.

I struggled with the concept for a while and finally realized that, indeed, I needed to make that decision. So, I kneeled at Mom's knee one day and she led me in the prayer for salvation.

The Gadget

One day, when I was just a little guy, I was in the Ten Cent Store with my mother and saw a gadget that caught my eye. I didn't know what it was but I wanted to examine it and maybe take it apart to study it. Mom was usually good about buying me a trinket, such as a little car or airplane, whenever we were in that store so I asked her if I could have the gadget. She was busy at the time, looking at something else, and told me that I didn't need it because it was a mousetrap. However, it didn't look like any mousetrap I had ever seen. I gave her a little while and then asked her again. She just said, "No." I thought about throwing a tantrum but quickly decided against that tactic. I had tried that once before and received a painful treatment with a hickory switch across the back of my thighs when we got home.

So, when no one was looking, I stuck the gadget in my pocket. I was still fascinated with the trap and was giving it a complete examination at home when I thought I was alone. I was so absorbed that I didn't notice Mom standing over me. She said, "Danny, where did you get that?" I was scared to lie so I replied, "At the Ten Cent Store." Then she handed me the pruning scissors and told me to go cut her a switch from the bush outside. I could already feel the pain but I complied with her orders and returned with the switch as slowly as I could get away with. When I handed her the shears and the stick, she said, " I've changed my mind. I believe that stealing needs a harder lesson and I have decided to let your father deal with it." I would have rather had her punishment.

I really hated for Dad to get home that evening. He usually punished me pretty severely with his belt and would always tell me before he started that it was going to hurt him more than me. I thought a lot about that statement and wondered if maybe he could let me whip him if it hurt the whipper more than the whipee. I knew better than to make that suggestion.

Mom waited until after supper to tell him that little Danny had been caught stealing. The wait made matters worse. I wanted to get away or at least get it over with. When Dad found out, he sat me on his knee and gave me a lecture about stealing and how it was breaking one of the Ten Commandments, which was pretty serious. However, he praised me for telling the truth about where I got the trap. Then he asked me what I thought my punishment should be. I replied that a good, hard spanking should do it.

Dad thought for a little while and then said, "No, you must take the trap back to the store and see the manager. Then you must give it to him and ask his forgiveness for stealing and tell him you will never do it again." I thought, "Wow, I'm really getting off easy!"

Two days went by before Dad could take me to the store. The more I anticipated the meeting with the manager, the more I dreaded it. On the way to the store, I asked Dad if I could just get the spanking instead of having to face the manager but he refused. We entered the store and he told me I needed to ask the clerk to see the manager. She kind of smiled and went to his office. When she returned, she told me that the manager was ready to see me. So, I marched back to his office with Dad following me. The manager knew Dad and greeted him warmly by name. Dad told me to say my little speech to the gentleman. My legs were like Jell-O!

I handed him the mousetrap and told him I was sorry for taking it. Then I asked him to please forgive me. He was very gracious and told me he forgave me and thanked me for returning it. When Dad and I returned home, he stood by my side while I kneeled and asked God to forgive me. I felt much better!

In retrospect, I think my parents handled the incident very appropriately and I have never been guilty of shoplifting since.

The Big Tents

Once in awhile, I would be riding my bike around the streets of Paris and see a group of men putting up a big tent. I would get all excited thinking maybe a circus was coming. However, I would find out it was just for a revival meeting. One afternoon, they were trying to put one up in a very high velocity wind and it was such a struggle. They would drive a stake, fasten a rope to it, and the wind would pull it out.

At one point, they lost complete control of the whole thing and it blew up against a fence. It was a good thing the fence stopped it because it could have ended up in the next county. I asked them why they just didn't wait until the wind settled down, and they told me it had to be put up immediately because the first meeting was that night. They finally got it erected but the canvas was loose as a goose.

170

My family sometimes went to those revival meetings, and at times, they got to be kind of a circus. There was always a preacher from a big city such as Indianapolis, St. Louis, Chicago, etc. This added greatly to the mystique of the whole business. To think, a high-class evangelist coming to the small town of Paris to conduct meetings in a tent. It seemed similar to God sending his only son to come to this tiny planet to save us from our sins.

The traveling preachers always seemed to be animated, a quality that appealed to kids. Once there was a very animated preacher with a baldhead. In the summer, the lights attracted a varied species such as June bugs, moths, mosquitoes, etc. On this particular night, the bugs became fascinated with the shine on the preacher's head and began swarming around it. Then he really became animated and I thought he would let out a string of cuss words at any moment. The people couldn't keep from laughing and he lost control of the crowd and left the stage. A local pastor with a full head of hair took the stage, regained control, and completed the service.

Of course, there was no such thing as bug repellent in those days, and sometimes the mosquitoes would come in swarms to the smorgasbord. At times the bug slapping got so bad that it almost sounded like a continuous applause.

There was always a lady playing the piano and you can imagine how out of tune they were from being hauled all over the country and sitting outside in high humidity. There was usually a man leading the hymns and a skinny lady singing a solo in a shrill voice.

A portable generator usually powered the lights, and power failures at a serious point in the sermon were common. People would sit in the dark in stunned silence but some of the more fired up preachers would go right on in the dark. They would usually break out the kerosene lanterns to provide illumination until the power was restored.

Once in awhile, a sudden, summer storm would vent its fury on a frail tent. Sometimes these were terrifying to the group of people huddled inside. Lightning would flash, thunder would crack and the canvas would snap. Then the rain would come down in torrents. Little kids would be crying and some adults would be praying for mercy. Maybe a violent storm had something to do with the decisions made at a few of the revival meetings.

Then there was the night when a pack of five or six dogs decided to come to the tent meeting. They ran in under the tent, did a quick look around and exited under the tent on the other side. This caused a mild stir and the preacher exclaimed, "Now, that's preachin' when you can even attract dogs!" They were probably just checking the place for a handout but quickly decided it was a poor place to get food, other than spiritual food.

As circus-like as some of these tent meetings were, they seemed to be effective, with people responding to the alter call while we sang the hymn, *"Just as I Am"* over and over until they stopped coming forward. One man in town kept going forward at every tent meeting and I asked Mom why he did this. She said that he obviously had a problem and needed to understand that you only had to be saved once.

The Schoolhouse Church

For a while, when I was a pre-teen, our family attended a weekly evening church service in a country schoolhouse. It was the only time that Dad faithfully attended church. He usually had other things that captured his interest such as fishing, hunting or going to shooting matches on Sundays, his only day off. He and the pastor, Vernon Denham, really hit it off and Dad enjoyed his preaching. I was thrilled to have him sit next to us in church and didn't argue about going.

In 1952, my sister was married to Joe Kurchak, who she met while attending Moody Bible Institute in Chicago. They were married at the

Methodist Church on North Central Avenue in Paris. Reverend Vernon Denham officiated at their wedding. My job, at the wedding, was to sit on the front row and record the ceremony on an old wire recorder, which was about as big as a suitcase.

Joe went on to graduate from Northern Baptist Seminary in Chicago and served for many years as a Baptist pastor in churches in Lake Geneva, Wisconsin and Milwaukee before changing careers in midlife. My sister was also able to earn postgraduate degrees in education and served many years in the school system in Boulder, Colorado. Their marriage produced four wonderful children, two boys and two girls.

The Hippodrome

When I was about 13, I suppose I was about as rebellious as I could be under Dad's strict hand. I didn't think much about God because I thought I was invincible, and really didn't think I needed God's help right then. I decided that I would put God on the back burner and call on him when I got old. That can be a fatal mistake that a lot of people make. He needs us to be dedicated believers while we are young and energetic. Also, we never know from one second to the next when we might step into eternity.

One day, my parents announced that we were going to go to a revival service at the Hippodrome Theater in Terre Haute. They seemed to take for granted that I was going with them. The Hippodrome was built in 1915 and was one of the earliest vaudeville theaters in the country. Al Jolson, Jack Benny and Ralph Bellamy performed there in its heyday. Plans are now underway to restore the old building to its former splendor.

Well, I thought that maybe the service would be similar to a tent meeting and I might be entertained. I was certainly entertained all right!

The evangelist was Curly Owens who had been a sparring partner for the famous boxer, Max Baer. (Check it out on Google.) He was the most dynamic preacher that I have ever witnessed, before or since. He would trot across the stage, emulating boxing movements while emphasizing scriptural points. As you can imagine, this was really fascinating to a thirteen year-old boy and I was spellbound.

Not only that, but he had the entire Bible memorized, old and new testaments from cover to cover! He claimed that God had given him the gift and he just woke up one day and knew it. We all wondered if he really knew the *whole* Bible, or just the passages he quoted. He would ask someone in the audience to yell out the book, chapter and number of a verse and; without hesitation, he would quote it word for word from the King James Version. He did this time after time at every one of the services we attended. It could not have been stooges yelling the verse numbers because some of the folks from our church participated and they vowed that it was not a set-up. *Amazing*!

Well, I was enchanted. After his last service, I came home, kneeled down beside my bed and rededicated my life to Christ. It was so wonderful to feel the presence of the Holy Spirit with me. I adopted two Bible verses as my lifelong favorites:

> *"For God so loved the world,*
> *that He gave His only begotten Son,*
> *that whosoever believeth in Him,*
> *should not perish, But have*
> *everlasting life."*
> John 3:16 (KJV)

> *"Jesus saith unto him: I am the*
> *way, the truth, and the life.*
> *No man cometh unto The Father,*
> *but by Me."*
> John 14:6 (KJV)

If Jesus Christ truly is who He claimed to be, and I believe He is, our most important duty on this earth is to get to know Him. Think about it. If He is not who He said He is, what have we got to lose if we do believe Him and simply live a quality life? On the other hand, if He truly is the Son of God and we reject Him, we must contemplate where we will spend eternity.

Setting the Example

I have been blessed all my life with some wonderful examples that have been set for me. I saw my father when he was awfully angry but I never heard him take the Lord's name in vain, not even once. He did not go beyond "hell" or "damn" when he was in the cursing mode. He didn't even say "s---."

When he was first married, he drank alcohol pretty regularly. He came home drunk one night, got sick and vomited on the floor. But he was sober enough to see Mom cleaning it up. That incident so disgusted him that he never once touched alcohol for the rest of his life. I never saw it cross his lips.

After we moved to the livestock farm on Sulphur Springs Road southeast of Paris in 1948, I helped some farmers in the hayfields around Redmon. They were a hard working bunch and every evening about dark, the owner of the farm where we happened to be working went to town and brought back a case of beer for the boys. I wondered how Dad would handle this when they got around to working on our farm near Redmon and filled the hayloft in the barn on the farm where we lived.

Finally, the day arrived. About sunset, Dad left for town and I wondered and wondered what he would bring back. If he just brought soft drinks, his name would forever be "mud" among those guys. After a while he drove up and unloaded a case of beer and two Cokes, one for him and one for me. While the guys were drinking beer, Dad sat there and "shot the bull" while he drank his

Coke. They never thought any less of him and my admiration for him soared to new heights. He was such a good storyteller that it probably helped everyone be at ease in this situation.

I am sorry to say that I have not lived up to Dad's standard at all points in my life, especially while in the Navy, but I always thought of him when I took a drink. I think that is why I never had a problem with drinking and could indulge or leave it alone. *Thanks, Dad*!

He was from the "old school" and made sure that his word was as good as his signature. I saw him make many deals, sometimes involving significant dollars, with just a handshake. Sometimes keeping his word cost him a lot of money but he always held to it. He also made sure he paid his bills on time, and didn't have a very high regard for those who didn't.

There have been many other people in my life who have set wonderful examples for me: my grandparents, my siblings, some friends, some of my co-workers, etc. As stated before, I have been well blessed in this regard.

It is *so important* to set good examples. Later in life, when I was scoutmaster for Boy Scout Troop 305, sponsored by the Fourth Avenue Methodist Church in Faribault, Minnesota, we included the following scripture in the training manual for new leaders:

> *"Let no man despise thy youth;*
> *but be thou an **example** of the believers,*
> *in word, in conversation,*
> *in charity, in spirit, in faith, in purity."*
> 1 Timothy 4:12 (KJV)

Conclusion

I began this book with a short discussion about boundaries and barriers and I will end it the same way. We need to be *very* careful with the boundaries and barriers we erect in our lives and other people's lives. So many folks make life so unpleasant and unfruitful by limiting themselves or others. Let me give you some examples.

I have a friend who was brought up in an orphanage. From the time he was a little tyke, he loved to peck around on the piano. When he was a little older, he started taking piano lessons but was having a struggle. One day, his teacher sat down next to him and said, "Dennis, you are doing so well. I just know that someday you will be a wonderful concert pianist."

Those two thoughtful sentences changed his life. She had removed his barrier and he really knuckled down and became a good pianist. He never became a concert performer, but enjoyed music and played the piano in church from time to time. What a wonderful liberation!

On the other hand, there was a young girl who loved to sing and was pretty good at it. One day, a careless person made this remark to her, "What makes you think you can sing?" What a terrible thing to say! The girl never tried to sing again. A barrier stronger than the *Gooseberry Hedge* had been erected in her life.

Some of us put barriers in our relationships that prevent others from getting close to us. Or we may establish boundaries that filter out those with certain characteristics. Maybe we draw the line at making friends with someone of another race or religion. Maybe we just don't like the appearance of a person or someone of another generation.

The thing we must be most careful about is erecting barriers between God and ourselves. I have, at times, put God on the back burner and would not let Him close to me where I live. He was not entirely missing but He was up against a filter boundary, which was backed up by a barrier. Looking back, those were the unhappiest times in my life. He wants to be our friend and be with us in our daily lives. He does not like boundaries or barriers and will sometimes act in drastic ways to remove them.

Also, instead of a barrier, we can install a sort of check valve. We can configure it so that we can reach out whenever we want, but others can't reach in. That can be really frustrating to others who want to be a part of our lives but are confused as to how to do it because they are getting mixed messages.

Well, it's time to wind this down. I have had more fun writing this than the law should allow. Thank you very much for being patient to the bitter end.

I am going to end this work with an epilogue consisting of a story I wrote in 2003 about a trip down a wild river with a troop of Boy Scouts in 1976. The reason I am tacking this on is to give you some examples of how God cares for us and how He can be with us in our daily lives.

Epilogue

On the Waters of the Sparkling Crow,
So That Doubters Will Know.
Divine Guidance to Show,
God Shines His Light
For Travelers Below.

The Author

On the Wings of a Crow

This is a story about a series of events that took place in 1976 while I was serving as scoutmaster for Troop 305 in Faribault, Minnesota. During the years since, I have thought about these events frequently because they have had such a profound influence on my life. Even though I had received Christ at an early age, I was bothered by doubts, sometimes even doubting the existence of a God that could control our lives on a daily basis even in small ways.

Up until 1976, my duties as a scoutmaster, I thought, were to keep the kids under control during meetings and to see that they received a positive experience from scouting. Looking back, I really knew little about what I was doing and would probably have been the first to admit it. Each summer, we leaders tried to see that the older boys could participate in some sort of a high adventure experience that they could look forward to with great anticipation that would keep them interested in scouting.

Epilogue

During the summer of 1975, our troop, along with some leaders and boys from another troop, had gone for about 10 days canoeing in the beautiful Boundary Waters Canoe Area on the Canadian-Minnesota border. But this beautiful pristine area will be the subject of another tale.

Sometime after the Boundary Waters trip, I realized that if I was to continue as scoutmaster, I needed more training. So in the spring of 1976, I was able to take the Woodbadge course. This is the highest level of training for scout leaders whereby you learn and practice eleven leadership skills in a wilderness environment. Upon completion of Woodbadge, in order to complete the requirements to receive your beads, neckerchief and slide, the prestigious symbols of a Woodbadger, you must draft and complete your "ticket."

A Woodbadge ticket involves the setting of goals as to how you are going to use your newly learned leadership skills in your scout leadership position, and then prove to your counselor that you had actually "worked your ticket."

When I drafted my ticket, many of my intended goals were to be worked during my troop's high adventure trip planned for the summer. My counselor approved this plan and I was very enthused about being a scout leader at this point in my career.

Troop 305's adventure for the summer of 1976 was to be a canoe trip down a wild and scenic river in Northern Minnesota named The Crow Wing. A caravan of parents would take us to a point upstream. Cars and pickups carrying an assortment of backpacks along with canoes on top and on trailers would wend their way to the starting point many miles north of Faribault near the town of Nimrod. There were approximately nine older scouters and five leaders and parents participating in this adventure. The drivers were instructed to meet us eight days later at a certain point about fifty miles downstream to load up for the trip back to Faribault and civilization. For those fifty miles on the river, we would be almost totally out of touch with the outside world, and would have to be at the appointed pick up spot at the appointed time.

Our volunteer guide was Bob Nichols who was also an advisor for our troop back in Faribault. Our scouting experiences contributed greatly toward Bob and I becoming best friends and we later enjoying many hours of hunting, sailing and just hanging out together. I would like to dedicate this story to the memory of him since he passed away in 1998. Our friendship and our experience together during the events on The Crow Wing had a very profound influence on my life. Another important participant on this trip was Assistant Scoutmaster, Louis Schuenke who has since passed. I have many fond memories of working with Louis through thick and thin leading the troop. He was a valuable asset to the troop and the scouts all loved him.

Day One....Sunday

Our troop was dropped off at a county park on the banks of the river where there was a nice public camping area. This camping area and the one planned for the next evening would be the only ones adjacent to county roads until the camp at the pick up point eight days later. The weather appeared to be threatening from the very beginning, with leaded skies and rolling clouds overhead. There were other campers in the park and much of the overheard conversation was about the weather.

We busied ourselves setting up camp and preparing the evening meal. The troop was separated into two patrols and each patrol had their own campsite and did their own cooking. The leaders would split up with some eating with each patrol. The boys took great pride in being able to cook for their adult guests. The weather was becoming more of a concern with each passing hour.

Epilogue

As part of my ticket, I had planned a church service for this Sunday evening to be held on the bank of the river at sunset. This was planned in detail with some of the scouts and the other leaders participating in the service. I was very concerned with the weather and thought we might have to have the service huddled in tents, which was certainly not the way I had envisioned it.

Sure enough, as we were cleaning up after supper it began to rain. Experienced campers will attest that few things can be more miserable than camping in the rain. It truly looked like it had set in for the night. However, church must go on. After the chores were done, I had the whole troop come together and prepared to have church in tents where we could hear each other through the fabric. This was not the best way to do church!

Just as we were gathering, the sky began to clear. It stayed clear which allowed us to gather on the riverbank with a beautiful sunset as a backdrop. Thus began a series of events that truly convinced me that God was in firm control of the situation.

As we were walking back from the river to our campsites it resumed raining. During the night, a violent storm blew in. Since we were not under any large trees, which could have fallen on us, and the lightning was somewhat distant, we stayed put in our tents as did the other campers nearby. However, the wind blew with great force so that our first night on the river was not too pleasant.

Day Two....Monday

We emerged from our tents that morning to a tangled sight that made it evident that a storm had visited us. The whole campground was in disarray with most of the tents of "civilian" campers blown down. All of the tents of our troop were still standing, a fact that many of the other campers noticed and commented on. They told us that we Boy Scouts certainly knew how to pitch tents. I began to realize that someone besides us was in control here.

After breakfast we loaded the canoes up and launched them into the sparkling Crow Wing. We had a rather uneventful morning seeing lots of wildlife along the river and stopping for sandwiches on the bank at noon. We made camp in the middle of the afternoon because I had planned some teaching events for the scouters to be done along the way. This was part of my Woodbadge ticket.

We were somewhat concerned with the water level in the river that we had observed during the day. It seemed as though the level was lower than we expected, the bottoms of the canoes just gliding over many large rocks that were on the bottom of the river. Louis Schuenke, the father of two of the boys on the trip, had just purchased a new aluminum canoe for the trip. He had polished the canoe to a mirror finish and was very proud of it. I think he believed that the craft would end the trip as pretty as it began. He expressed his concern about the rocks he was barely missing as the canoe went along. He had not seen anything yet!

This being our bicentennial year, I had planned some teaching problems for the troop with a revolutionary war theme. For example, each patrol was to build a tower out of poles about 12-15 feet tall for Paul Revere to observe the coming of the British troops. The instructions included a colorful tale of the struggle for independence and how important it was to build a tower. The guys really got into the spirit of the thing, and each patrol built a great tower. The leaders judged the structures and awarded appropriate rustic prizes for first and second places.

Our trip was going great and I was pleased that work on my ticket was going according to plan. We retired to camp to finish setting up and cooking the evening meal. There was much discussion during the meal about the building of the towers and how they could have done it better. I was pleased to see that everyone seemed to be having a good time.

Epilogue

When we finished cleaning up after supper, we walked a short distance to a county park where the mother of the Bauernfeind boys was to bring the rest of the family to take part in our campfire experience. This was to be the last point where we would be near a county road where we could have visitors. From here on the river would be going through wilderness country, and contact with the outside world would be very difficult if not impossible.

Traditionally at each campfire service, after a good time of singing and telling stories, I would present a scoutmaster's minute where I would relate something serious and inspirational for the boys to think about as they prepared for bed. For this evening I had planned to tell the story of how they trapped monkeys by cutting a small hole in a gourd and filling it with seeds. When they left it hanging in a tree, a monkey would come up and put his hand through the hole to grasp a handful of seeds. However, his hand in a fist would not pass through the hole to bring the seeds out. The monkey was too greedy to let go of the seeds, and would stay there until he could be captured. This was to illustrate that it was not good to be greedy.

Just a few minutes before the monkey story, the visiting little brother of Jeff and Mike Bauernfeind told his mother he had to go back to their vehicle to get something. He brought back a toy monkey! I swear that I had not told anyone what the scoutmaster minute would be about. This really blew my mind! So, before I started the monkey story, I went over to the boy and asked to borrow the monkey and held it up while I told the story. This appeared to the scouts as though I had just thought of the monkey story after I saw the monkey.

I just realized that maybe I was right in believing that someone else could be in control here.

We all slept well that night with thoughts of traveling the beautiful Crow Wing filling our heads.

Day Three....Tuesday

We stayed in that area until about noon. There was another teaching problem for the scouts as soon as our pancake breakfast was over. The problem consisted of guiding the Revolutionary troops through the woods with a map and compass to find the British camp, so that they could conduct a surprise attack. This was good orienteering training, and everyone seemed to enjoy it. Then we launched our canoes.

It must have been sometime in the middle of the afternoon when the Schuenke canoe scraped over the first rock. It must have made quite a sound because I looked over at their canoe. Louis was obviously in great pain to think about what the bottom of that canoe would look like. He had just polished it after they beached it the evening before.

The further we went, the worse the conditions became: more rocks and lower water level. We had to make good time because we had just started after noon and had to stay on schedule in order to get picked up at the appointed time and place.

Then all the canoes began hitting rocks and some would even lodge on one and spin in the current until someone would get out of the canoe and drag it free, or another passing canoe would tow it off the rock. We were, however, able to travel the required distance that afternoon.

During an afternoon break on the riverbank, Louis pulled his canoe out of the water to inspect the bottom. He was sick at heart because there were many scratches and a few shallow dents. I asked him if we could go on a little walk in the woods together because I needed to talk. I told him I realized he was proud of the new canoe and how he and his sons had saved up for it. "But," I said, "it could still be in perfect condition hanging in their garage if he had not brought his boys on this trip that they would always remember."

Epilogue

My talk must have done some good because his attitude completely changed and they would actually laugh from then on when
they hit rocks. He pulled his canoe alongside mine and said to me,
"This canoe will always show that it took quite a trip, won't it,
Hall?"

That evening we made camp and had a meal of bullhead catfish
that were caught from the river. Everyone bathed in the river and
felt refreshed for the campfire that evening. We really felt like ad-
venturers.

It was about midnight when the little guy woke Mr. Schuenke up
because he had a pain in his stomach. He began throwing up and
everything was a mess even before the diarrhea started. Louis had
quite a job cleaning him up along with his sleeping bag. We did
have a first aid kit along so Louis gave him some medicine to settle
his stomach. The boy told him that his sister had the stomach flu
just before he left for the trip.

I knew nothing about this until the next morning.

Day Four....Wednesday

On Wednesday morning, the boy with the flu was still exhibit-
ing fairly severe symptoms. Even though he had very little ap-
petite, we made sure to keep him hydrated the best we could.
We also did our best to keep him isolated from the other members of the troop.

Some of the scouts expressed the desire to learn more about the
map and compass, so Bob Nichols worked with them on learning
some of the finer points. The remainder of the troop wanted free
time, so some went fishing; others went swimming and some just
hung out. Some of the guys said that they did not feel very well.

After a light lunch we launched the canoes to resume our trip downstream. The situation with the low water level had not improved and some of the guys became a little disgruntled from the rough going over the rocks. Bob Nichols told me that we would run into what would normally be light rapids before the trip was over, and wondered what they would be like with the low water conditions. We tried not to think about it. If necessary, we could portage around them, which would be a chore. As the afternoon wore on, the complaints about not feeling well became more numerous.

About the time we arrived at camp in the late afternoon, the flu was beginning to manifest itself with all its fury. Several of the boys, as well as some of the adults, were complaining and a few had begun to throw up. I did not feel too well myself, but thought that it could be from the power of suggestion. We adult leaders had a pow-wow to discuss our options under the present circumstances. We certainly did not want to put the troop at risk of becoming so ill that it would endanger them. We reasoned that we were so far from civilization that it would take one day of solid canoeing and another one-half day to flag a car and travel to a medical facility to get help. Since the boy who first had the symptoms was getting a little better, we decided to let the flu run its course, treating it as best we could, and proceed.

I would rather not elaborate on the events of that night. It was very bad! Very little sleep was enjoyed by anyone. The dawn revealed many sleeping bags hung up to dry from being washed in the river during the night. Louis Schuenke assumed the role of troop medic and did a wonderful job. His sleeping bag-side manner was something to behold and he instilled a sense of confidence in everyone he came into contact with. Talk about an encourager!

Epilogue

Day Five....Thursday

Those who felt like having breakfast ate, but many did not even want to look at food. I had planned another teaching problem for the scouts but abandoned that idea due to the condition of the troop and the fact that, to stay on schedule, we had to spend more time on the river that day. Much of the morning was spent just caring for the sick. This must have been a potent variety of the flu since virtually everyone on the trip was affected to varying degrees. I felt terrible myself but tried not to let on too much.

That afternoon on the river was another experience I do not care to be too graphic about, but it was mean. We placed a forked stick in the stern of each canoe upon which we hung a roll of toilet paper. Every once in awhile, a canoe would head for the bank with one or two of the passengers jumping out and heading to the woods with the TP roll. Occasionally they would be in such a hurry they would forget the TP and someone in the canoe would throw them a long football type pass with the roll. If we had not all felt so terrible, it would have been funny. We certainly spread a goodly amount of fertilizer along the way that day.

We made camp late that evening and even skipped the campfire since we were all hurting so bad. Those who could eat, ate while most just turned in to try to get some sleep. The night passed somehow.

Day Six....Friday

Dawn found us in terrible shape! It was the custom on the trip that a morning mustering in would be held each day. The scouts would all stand at attention as their names were called so that all would be accounted for. Then myself or another leader would give them a review of the planned activities for the day and what could be expected.

This morning found the scouts too weak to comfortably stand up, so I let them sit on the grass during the muster. I could hardly stand up myself. I wondered if this was kind of how Washington's troops felt like at Valley Forge. I expressed my thought to them and someone made the remark that maybe I was carrying this 1776 theme a little too far. It was good to know that our senses of humor were not entirely lost.

Then something happened that to this day I have never been able to explain. I had never before experienced anything like it nor have I in the 27 years since.

I wanted to say something that would encourage the adults as well as the scouts, because I knew how difficult it was to even be there. I also knew that this would be the toughest day on the river with many miles to cover, and the rapids still looming ahead. I also knew that no one even felt like getting into a canoe, let alone spending the entire day with a paddle in their hands.

I saw Bob Nichols' camp ax leaning against the base of a tree and got the urge to pick it up. From then on during the muster, I experienced a sort of out-of-body sensation. I really was not in control of my actions or speech. Here is the best I can do in remembering a part of it.

I removed the leather cover from the ax while the rest of the troop and their leaders observed. I examined it and began to speak. "Here is a fine looking ax and I can see that it has been used and been sharpened at least once but I don't really know about the quality of it. We could only test the metal by using it. Then we would know about the quality of this ax, how well it holds an edge, how it is balanced, how it swings, etc. Today, we will have our mettle tested on that river. We have a long way to go and we all know the conditions facing us. There are rapids up ahead through which we must navigate or portage around and it will be a long day even if we felt better.

Epilogue

Now, we can make it as miserable as we can for our companions, and ourselves or we can rise up and make the most of the situation and remain cheerful throughout the ordeal. And don't forget that 'cheerful' is one of the points of the Scout Law. Now let us begin our longest day." At this point, I was welcomed back into my body.

Since that day I have heard of similar things happening to other leaders where they seemed to be used by someone else speaking through them but that was my only experience with it. I must say that it was rather disconcerting but not altogether unpleasant, more like fascinating.

There seemed to be a remarkable change in the ranks and they really appeared to get in the spirit of preparing for what lay ahead. Tents were taken down, sleeping bags rolled up, packs were packed, canoes were launched, and off we went.

Without going into great detail, it truly was a long day. But things seemed to go better as we went. The water level in the river was a little higher, the sun was bright and cheerful, we all began to feel better; and most remarkable of all, everyone remained in a good mood, even teasing each other again.

To prepare for the rapids, we instructed the paddlers that they must keep the canoes moving faster than the water was moving in order to be able to steer around rocks and boulders in the rapids. Most of them knew this by now.

We could hear them before we arrived. Somehow, we made it through with only one canoe capsizing. This was not a big problem because the boys climbed up on a fallen tree trunk while we all pitched in to rescue them and the canoe, and to gather up all the equipment floating downstream.

We were all very weary when we finally beached the canoes at the appointed campsite. Then there were the usual chores of setting up camp, finding firewood, building fires, cooking the evening meal, cleaning up afterward, etc. When we said Grace over supper, we all felt truly grateful.

We cut our campfire short that evening. The stories that were told were mostly about the experiences with the rapids. One of the boys expressed the desire to take a trip down a wilder river with more whitewater. The others nodded their heads in agreement. At this point, I knew that the flu bug was history. Praise the LORD!

We all fell into our sleeping bags that evening and didn't know a thing until morning.

Day Seven....Saturday

Early Saturday morning I met with Bob Nichols, our guide. We reviewed the day's route and the planned camping area for our last night on the river. He pointed out that we could camp at a different spot a little further downstream, and be closer to the point where we were to be picked up on Sunday afternoon. I agreed to this change in plans with the understanding that we should arrive at this unscheduled campsite early enough to be able to achieve all that I had planned for the evening.

I really wanted to make the last night something memorable for the scouts. I had planned a special campfire where we would sing, do skits, and tell stories just as usual, but finish with a really touching time where we would go on a Scout Law walk. A Scout Law walk is where you have posted signs in the woods with one point of the Scout Law on each sign. Then a leader would lead the walk, illuminating each sign with a candle while he read the meaning of each of the twelve points. We had brought along a couple of brown Sharpies to write on the signs. This would kind of look like the words had been burned into the wood.

Epilogue

Here are the points of the Scout Law: A scout is *Trustworthy, Loyal, Helpful, Friendly, Courteous, Kind, Obedient, Cheerful, Thrifty, Brave, Clean, and Reverent.* Other than the Bible, I have found the Scout Law to be a very helpful guide to living a quality life. I remember each point and the order in which they are stated after all those years since I memorized them as a scout.

As the leader on the Scout Law walk would come to each sign, he would read the explanation as written in the Boy Scout Manual. For Example: "*Thrifty*...A scout works to pay his way and to help others. He protects and conserves natural resources. He carefully uses his time and property."

Well, off we went that morning after breakfast and mustering in. This was a much different mustering in scene than the one earlier. Spirits were high and I could feel there was growing anticipation of getting back to Faribault and civilization. One scout said that the thing he missed most was the Dairy Queen. Most allowed that what they missed most was TV.

We had a rather uneventful day on the river. We took a long lunch and played some games and just hung out for a while. I had mixed emotions about returning home. Sure I had missed being home and would be happy to be back, but then I would miss the river and all the guys on the trip. It had been an interesting experience that I knew I would never forget.

We arrived at our campsite about mid-afternoon. I climbed up the hill from the river to behold something that made me do a double take. There was the most beautiful wilderness campfire facility that I had ever laid eyes on. There was a masonry ring about 20 feet in diameter constructed of river stones. It had a flat stone top that would serve as a seat for many people. In the middle of the ring was a place for the fire with the wood already laid for a large fire. It was like someone was expecting us and wanted to make things as comfortable as possible for us.

Here is the unbelievable part. Piled against the ring were 12 saw-mill planks about 24" long and 10" wide. These were no doubt left there for burning but they would be perfect for the signs to be used in our Scout Law walk. Bob Nichols marveled at this sight also, and to think that we were not originally scheduled to stop here. This was about the time he said to me, "It is obvious that someone is looking after us on this trip." I had to agree wholeheartedly.

That afternoon we gave the boys free time for swimming, playing games and just being boys. It was obvious they were excited about getting home. I wish their parents, who were not with us, could have seen them. Here the river was deeper and more suitable for swimming and most of us really enjoyed it. Someone had to keep an eye on the swimmers, which we required for safety, so we took turns at that detail.

Supper that evening found us cleaning up leftovers from the previous meals on the trip, nothing gourmet to be sure. One of the leaders treated us to a desert of pineapple upside-down cake baked in a Dutch oven. Mmmmm…Good!

After cleaning up the mess from the meal, we prepared for the campfire, which was to be sort of a graduation ceremony for those scouts who had never been on one of our high adventure trips. We would all have earned the 50 Miler Paddling Award, which would be awarded at the next Court of Honor. We had made sure that we had traveled at least 50 miles on the river.

We gathered at the fire ring about sunset with the fire already burning. We told the usual stories, sang good old scout songs, did some skits, etc. Then we gave each boy the assignment of picking another boy and telling about him. It had to be a different person each time and all the comments had to be positive. This was new to them and they struggled with it.

After dark, we went on the Scout Law walk through the woods and it was very solemn. We had each person, scouts and leaders, return to the campfire with a small pine twig with the needles intact. After we settled around the fire in the darkness, each person in turn would approach the fire with his twig. He would hold the twig and tell what this trip had meant to him and what he had learned from it. Then he would cast the twig upon the embers and meditate while it flared up and burned. I remember that several of the scouts mentioned that they learned about overcoming adversity. We all learned something about that! My scoutmaster minute that evening elaborated upon that very point.

Although the boys were serious during the last part of the campfire ceremony, when they got back to their tents, they got a little rowdy. This was to be expected since this was to be their last night in tents for a while. The leaders dealt with it and we finally got to sleep sometime after midnight.

Day Eight....Sunday

The only thing remaining to do was to get everyone awake, have breakfast, clean up, break camp, load the canoes, have a brief devotion, and head for our pick-up point for the trip home. I began to feel a little relieved. It is a big responsibility being in charge of a group like this for a wilderness trip. So many things could happen and I felt blessed that all we had to deal with was the flu and the low water. It would be a relief to turn the boys back over to their parents.

We loaded up and paddled down-river to the pick up site and had lunch while we waited on the vehicles.

The trip back to Faribault was uneventful. The boys were feeling let down, so most of them slept on the way.

Conclusion

There you have it. I related this story as best I could remember after all these years. Some of the minor events may be slightly distorted but I do not doubt my memory as far as the sequence of the profound events and the exact happenings. I have thought too much about them to ever forget. This trip was discussed for years afterward among the leaders and the boys.

This, for me, was a very remarkable experience and I felt that I was being held in the palm of God's hand for one week. It was a glorious feeling, one that has never been duplicated exactly. It was proven to me beyond the shadow of a doubt that God does indeed exist and He is willing to help us if we will just call on Him. He does not keep us from all adversity but through it all, He is there for us to call upon.

> *"And we know that all things*
> *work together for good to them*
> *that love God, to them who are*
> *called according to His purpose."*
> Romans 8:28 (KJV)

> *"... for He hath said, I will never*
> *leave thee, nor forsake thee."*
> Hebrews 13:5 (KJV)

I believe that God has a special place in His heart for those who work with children and youth and for one special week; I reaped the benefits of His divine attention.

We were all very happy to receive the 50-Miler patch at the Court of Honor that autumn. We knew what it took to earn it.

Even though the adversity kept me from completing my Wood-badge ticket on just that trip, I was able to finish it later and was

Epilogue

awarded my Baden Powell beads, neckerchief, and slide. I keep them in a safe place.

Louis Schuenke's oldest son, Scott, fulfilled the requirements for Eagle that year and we held an Eagle Court of Honor for him. It was a beautiful ceremony done on the bicentennial theme.

I would like to have the opportunity to learn about the lives of each of those boys since they participated in that canoe trip so long ago. I think of them often. One thing I am relatively sure of is that they have not forgotten the events of that summer on the Crow Wing.

References

Postwar Economy

www.scaruffi.com/politics/dow.html

www.thepeoplehistory.com/1946.html

www.mclib.info/prices/1946.html

Paris Basketball

http://books.google.com/books?id=QS19Rcb6DAYC&pg=PA
16&lpg=PA16&dq=ernie+eveland+paris+il&source=web&ots
=JwhICITmwy&sig=BXV2iZIlnY-
6aXShDNmBtUnJy6w#PPA16,M1

The Island Queen

www.cincinnati.com/tallstacks/ts_onboard_island.html

Hit Songs, 1946

www.trivia-library.com/b/billboard-top-5-pop-singles-
1946.htm

Best Movies, 1946

www.moviegoods.com/dyn_browseYear.asp?ryear=1946

References

World War II Tank Production

http://en.wikipedia.org/wiki/M4_Sherman

http://www.2worldwar2.com/german-tanks.htm

Lend-Lease Program

http://en.wikipedia.org/wiki/Lend-Lease

The Hippodrome Theater

http://mastermason.com/aasr-valley-of-terre-haute/a-history.htm

www.ingramcontent.com/pod-product-compliance
Lightning Source LLC
Chambersburg PA
CBHW021053090426
42738CB00006B/316